THE GREATEST LIFE

THE GREATEST LIFE

Jesus Tells His Story

FRANK C. LAUBACH

FLEMING H. REVELL COMPANY

INTRODUCTION

LET JESUS HIMSELF TELL THE STORY

Many of us remember the delight with which, as children, we first read or heard read the Gospels, and met Jesus face to face. Here was the most gripping drama in the world! It sometimes made us weep. This joy may persist with the second reading and the third. But the time comes when our intense response diminishes. We find ourselves reading by rote, repeating words without realizing what we are saying. We fail any longer to experience the fresh, sweet joy which we felt when we first read the marvelous story. This, to be sure, is true of any book we read many times. But it must *not* be true of the story of Jesus, for here is the most important news for time and for eternity. We must find ways of sustaining the rapture and glory which we first felt.

I, for one, have been seeking fresh approaches to Jesus that would not only preserve but would intensify the intimacy and power of my awareness of His living presence. Like the rest of you, I did not want the picture to fade; I wanted it to become more vivid. I wanted Christ, the loveliest person who ever lived, to fill my very life. This book is the latest and for me the most glorious new adventure in getting closer to Him. Here, if you are anything like I am, you are going to have what the theologians call "a tremendous encounter" with the living Christ. Here He tells His own story.

Every Christian believes that in the Bible God talks to us.

[5]

That is what we mean when we call it "the Word of God." One day, while reading Goodspeed's translation, I thought, "Why not put this Gospel story into the first person? Let Jesus say 'I' instead of reading 'He.' Let Him tell the whole story Himself." The result was electric. It was appropriate. I went on and on, intrigued and sometimes in rapture, until all the four Gospels were written like an autobiography of Jesus. Here I found the most glorious realization of the living Christ I had ever known. It was what I had wanted for forty years and had never found so completely before.

I was fortunate enough to have my introduction to Jesus while sitting on my mother's knee, listening to her read a book called *Child's Bible Stories*. When she began to fall asleep, I would shake her chin until she read again. In my early teens I was fascinated by the big family Bible, crowded as it was with exciting pictures—Adam and Eve being driven out of the Garden of Eden, and on to John's superb visions on the island of Patmos. Gradually I came to understand that the supreme event of the Bible and of all the ages was the life and death and resurrection of Jesus Christ. This I read over and over and over until I knew the King James Version almost by heart.

The English in the King James Version of 1611 is marvelously beautiful, and yet it is four centuries old, and sometimes difficult to understand. It seems to relegate Jesus to the distant past, while our souls crave and need a Christ who lives today and speaks our language. This is why the many translations which have appeared in this century have had such a large reading. We read them to get more light, but I think we like them especially for the strong sense they give us that He walks among us and speaks to us now.

So millions of us have read the English Version of 1881, the American Version of 1901, the Twentieth Century Bible, the Weymouth and Moffat and Goodspeed and Williams and Knox and Phillips versions and translations. The Revised Standard Version of 1946 is the most widely read of the modern versions and has the largest agreement of scholars.

A great many of us also buy the true and fictional "Lives" of Jesus, in a constant effort to know more about the most

[6]

magnetic and unescapable person the world has ever seen. Jesus is so all-important, at times so close, and yet so inscrutable! I liked Papini's *Life of Christ* the best. Yet every life ever written is inferior to the Gospel stories. After all, everything written by any other than one of the four evangelists depends for its validity upon the original Gospels and the letters of The New Testament.

Many scholars have made strenuous efforts to peer behind the Gospels "in quest of the historic Jesus," but their writings leave the heart cold. What sets us on fire is the quest of the living Christ *today*, as a present, invisible Friend and Lord. That is why I am one of the millions who like pictures of Christ in my Bible and on the walls of my home. I like them on every wall, so that no matter where I turn there I see Him. You may object that nobody knows what Jesus looked like. I know, and yet . . . if those words of St. Paul, "Christ liveth in me," are true of some people today, He should be shining out through their faces if He dwells in their souls. So blond or brunette and Japanese or Indian or African pictures of Christ are all true if He lives within their hearts.

One of the best ways to realize Christ within you this minute is to imagine yourself walking with His disciples, and to walk with Him through the chapter you happen to be reading. For example, you may walk with them through Matthew 15 and you may say:

"Jesus, I see you landing from the boat at Gennesaret; some Pharisees are coming down the road from Jerusalem. They are walking up to you and saying, 'Why do your disciples transgress the tradition of the elders, for they do not wash their hands when they eat?' " Then the Gospel tells you what Jesus replied.

I was doing that one day when it suddenly burst upon me that He Himself is talking to us from these pages. It became vividly clear when I changed "He" to "I"; it instantly became personal and exciting, for it came straight from the lips of Jesus. Here I found the most glorious experience of the living Christ I have ever known.

I have selected Professor Goodspeed's translation as the basis of this "autobiography" because it is so dignified and

[7]

yet so human. I have pieced the four Gospels into one continuous story by following the sequence used in most of the "harmonies" of the Gospels. You will find here a verse quoted from Matthew, and there a verse from Mark or Luke or John, whichever gives the most complete story of each incident. Professor Goodspeed has given his hearty approval to this use of his translation, and so have his publishers, The University of Chicago Press.

There are no verse references or numbers to interrupt the reader's progress, but if you care to check you will find them accurately quoted from all the four Gospels.

None of this supposed "autobiography" has ever been printed in book form. Some of it appeared in the Benton *Argus,* a weekly newspaper in my home town in Pennsylvania. The editor of that newspaper has given his enthusiastic permission to reprint it here.

Now let Jesus Himself tell His story.

F. C. L.

HOW GABRIEL
ANNOUNCED JOHN'S BIRTH

In the days when Herod was king of Judea, there was a priest named Zechariah who belonged to the division of Abijah. His wife was also a descendant of Aaron, and her name was Elizabeth. They were both upright in the sight of God, blamelessly observing all the Lord's commands and requirements. They had no children, for Elizabeth was barren; and they were both advanced in life.

Once when he was acting as priest before God, when his division was on duty, it fell to his lot, according to the priests' practice, to go into the sanctuary of the Lord and burn the incense, while all the throng of people was outside, praying at the hour of the incense offering. And an angel of the Lord appeared to him, standing at the right of the altar of incense. When Zechariah saw him he was startled and overcome with fear. And the angel said to him,

"Do not be afraid, Zechariah, for your prayer has been heard. Your wife Elizabeth will bear you a son, and you are to name him John. This will bring gladness and delight to you, and many will rejoice over his birth. For he will be great in the sight of the Lord. He will drink no wine nor strong drink, but he will be filled with the holy Spirit from his very birth, and he will turn many of Israel's descendants to the Lord their God. He will go before him with the spirit and the power of Elijah, to reconcile fathers to their children, and to bring the disobedient back to the wisdom of upright men, to make a people perfectly ready for the Lord."

Zechariah said to the angel, "How am I to know that this is so? For I am an old man, and my wife is advanced in life."

The angel answered, "I am Gabriel. I stand in the very presence of God. I have been sent to speak to you and to tell you this good news. Now you will keep silent and be unable to speak until the day when this happens, because you have not

[9]

believed what I have said, for it will all be fulfilled in due time."

The people were waiting for Zechariah, and wondering that he stayed so long in the sanctuary. But when he came out he could not speak to them, and they knew that he had seen a vision in the sanctuary. For his part, he kept making signs to them, and remained dumb. And when his period of service was over, he went back to his home.

Soon afterward his wife Elizabeth began to expect a child, and she kept herself in seclusion for five months. "This is what the Lord has done for me," she said, "now that he has deigned to remove the disgrace I have endured."

HOW GABRIEL ANNOUNCED MY BIRTH

In the sixth month the angel Gabriel was sent by God to a town in Galilee called Nazareth, to my future mother, a maiden who was engaged to be married to a man named Joseph, a descendant of David. The maiden's name was Mary. And the angel went to her and said, "Good morning, favored woman! The Lord be with you!"

But she was startled at what he said, and wondered what this greeting meant. And the angel said to her,

"Do not be afraid, Mary, for you have gained God's approval. You are to become a mother and you will give birth to a son, and you are to name him Jesus. He will be great and will be called the Son of the Most High. The Lord God will give him the throne of his forefather David, and he will reign over Jacob's house forever; his reign will have no end."

Mary said to the angel, "How can this be, when I have no husband?" The angel answered, "The Holy Spirit will come over you, and the power of the Most High will overshadow you. For that reason your child will be called holy, and the Son of God. And your cousin Elizabeth, although she is old, is going to give birth to a son, and this is the sixth month with her who was said to be barren. For nothing is ever impossible for God."

And Mary said, "I am the Lord's slave. Let it be as you say."
Then the angel left her.

Mary's Visit to Her Cousin

In those days Mary, who was to become my mother, set
out and hurried to the hill-country, to a town in Judah, and
she went to Zechariah's house and greeted Elizabeth. When
Elizabeth heard Mary's greeting, the babe stirred within her.
And Elizabeth was filled with the holy Spirit and she gave a
great cry, and said,

"You are the most favored of women,
  And blessed is your child!
Who am I,
To have the mother of my Lord come to me?

"For the moment your greeting reached my ears,
  The child stirred with joy within me!
Blessed is she who has believed,
For what the Lord has promised her will be fulfilled!"

And Mary said,

"My heart extols the Lord,
  My spirit exults in God my Savior.
For he has noticed his slave in her humble station,
For from this time all the ages will think me favored!

"For the Almighty has done wonders for me,
  How holy his name is!
He shows his mercy age after age
To those who fear him.

"He has done mighty deeds with his arm,
  He has routed the proud-minded,

[11]

He has dethroned monarchs and exalted the poor.
He has satisfied the hungry with good things and sent the rich
   away empty-handed.

"He has helped his servant Israel,
   Remembering his mercy,
   As he promised our forefathers
   To have mercy on Abraham and his descendants forever!"

So my mother Mary stayed with her about three months, and
then returned home.

Birth of John the Baptist

Now the time came for Elizabeth's child to be born, and
she gave birth to a son. Her neighbors and relatives heard of
the great mercy the Lord had shown her, and they came and
congratulated her. On the eighth day they came to circumcise
her child, and they were going to name him Zechariah, after
his father. But his mother said,
   "No! He is to be named John."
They said to her,
   "There is no one among your relatives who bears that
name."
But they made signs to the child's father and asked him what
he wished to have the child named. He asked for a writing
tablet, and wrote,
   "His name is John."
And they were all amazed. Then his voice and the use of
his tongue were immediately restored, and he blessed God
aloud. And all their neighbors were overcome with fear, and
all over the hill-country of Judea all these stories were told,
and everyone who heard them kept them in mind, and said,
   "What is this child going to be?" For the Lord's hand was
with him.

The Song of Zechariah

And his father Zechariah was filled with the holy Spirit and he uttered a divine message, saying,

"Blessings on the Lord, the God of Israel,
Because he has turned his attention to his people, and brought about their deliverance,
And he has produced a mighty Savior for us
In the house of his servant David.

"By the lips of his holy prophets he promised of old to do this—
To save us from our enemies and from the hands of all who hate us,
Thus showing mercy to our forefathers,
And keeping his sacred agreement,

"And the oath that he swore to our forefather Abraham,
That we should be delivered from the hands of our enemies,
And should serve him in holiness and uprightness, unafraid,
In his own presence all our lives.

"And you, my child, will be called a prophet of the Most High,
For you will go before the Lord to make his way ready,
Bringing his people the knowledge of salvation
Through the forgiveness of their sins.

"Because the heart of our God is merciful,
And so the day will dawn upon us from on high,
To shine on men who sit in darkness and the shadow of death,
And guide our feet into the way of peace."

My cousin John grew up and became strong in the Spirit, and he lived in the desert until the day when he proclaimed himself to Israel.

My Birth and Infancy

Now these were the circumstances of my birth. Mary, my mother, was engaged to Joseph, but before they were married it was found that she was about to become a mother through the influence of the holy Spirit. But my father, Joseph, was an upright man and did not wish to disgrace her, and he decided to break off the engagement privately. But while he was thinking of doing this, an angel of the Lord appeared to him in a dream, and said,

"Joseph, descendant of David, do not fear to take Mary, your wife, to your home, for it is through the influence of the holy Spirit that she is to become a mother. She will have a son, and you are to name him Jesus, for it is he who is to save his people from their sins."

All this happened in fulfilment of what the Lord said through the prophet,

"The maiden will be pregnant and will have a son,
And they will name him Immanuel"

—a word which means "God with us." So when my father awoke from his sleep, he did as the angel of the Lord had directed him, and took Mary his wife to his home. But he did not live with her as a husband until I was born, and he named me Jesus.

In those days an edict was issued by the Emperor Augustus that a census of the whole world should be taken. It was the first census, taken when Quirinius was governor of Syria. So everyone went to his own town to register. And Joseph went up from Galilee from the town of Nazareth to Judea to the city of David called Bethlehem, because he belonged to the house and family of David, to register with my mother Mary, who was engaged to him and who was soon to become a mother. While they were there, the time came for me to be born, and she gave birth to me, her first-born son; and she wrapped me up, and laid me in a manger, for there was no room for us at the inn.

The Angels and the Shepherds

There were some shepherds in that neighborhood keeping watch through the night over their flock in the open fields. And an angel of the Lord stood by them, and the glory of the Lord shone around them, and they were terribly frightened. The angel said to them,

"Do not be frightened, for I bring you good news of a great joy that is to be felt by all the people, for today, in the town of David, a Savior for you has been born who is your Messiah and Lord. And this will prove it to you: You will find a baby wrapped up and lying in a manger."

Suddenly there appeared with the angel a throng of the heavenly army, praising God, saying,

> "Glory to God in heaven and on earth!
> Peace to the men he favors!"

When the angels left them and returned to heaven, the shepherds said to one another,

"Come! Let us go over to Bethlehem, and see this thing that has happened, that the Lord has told us of!"

And they hurried there, and found Mary my mother, and Joseph, with me lying in the manger. When they saw me, they told what had been said to them about me. And all who heard it were amazed at what the shepherds told them, but my mother treasured up all they had said, and pondered over it. And the shepherds went back glorifying God and praising him for all that they had heard and seen in fulfilment of what they had been told.

[15]

My Circumcision

When I was eight days old and it was time to circumcise me, I was named Jesus, as the angel had named me, before my birth was first expected.

The Presentation in the Temple

When their purification period under the Law of Moses was over, they took me up to Jerusalem to present me to the Lord, in fulfilment of the requirement of the Law of the Lord, "Every first-born male shall be considered consecrated to the Lord," and to offer the sacrifice prescribed in the Law of the Lord, "A pair of turtle-doves or two young pigeons."

Now there was a man in Jerusalem named Symeon, an upright, devout man, who was living in expectation of the comforting of Israel, and under the influence of the holy Spirit. It had been revealed to him by the holy Spirit that he should not die without seeing the Lord's Messiah. And under the Spirit's influence he went into the Temple, and when my parents brought me there to do for me what the Law required, Symeon also took me in his arms and blessed God, and said,

"Now, Master, you will let your slave go free
In peace, as you promised,
For my eyes have seen your salvation
Which you have set before all the nations,
A light of revelation for the heathen,
And a glory to your people Israel!"

My father and mother were astonished at what Symeon said about me. And he gave them his blessing, and said to Mary, my mother,

"This child is destined to cause the fall and rise of many in Israel, and to be a portent that will be much debated—you yourself will be pierced to the heart—and so the thoughts of many minds will be revealed."

There was also a prophetess there named Hannah, the daughter of Phanuel, who belonged to the tribe of Asher. She was very old, for after her girlhood she had been married for seven years, and she had been a widow until she was now eighty-four. She never left the Temple, but worshiped night and day with fasting and prayer. She came up just at that time and gave thanks to God and spoke about me to all who were living in expectation of the liberation of Jerusalem.

The Visit of the Wise Men

Now after my birth at Bethlehem in Judea, in the days of King Herod, astrologers from the east arrived at Jerusalem, and asked,

"Where is the newly born king of the Jews? For we have seen his star rise and we have come to do homage to him."

When King Herod heard of this, he was troubled, and all Jerusalem with him. So he called together all the high priests and scribes of the people and asked them where I was to be born. They said,

"At Bethlehem in Judea, for this is what the prophet wrote:
" 'And you, Bethlehem in Judah's land,
 You are by no means least important among the leading
  places of Judah,
 For from you will come a leader
 Who will be the shepherd of my people Israel.' "

Then Herod secretly sent for the astrologers, and found out from them the exact time when the star appeared. And he sent them to Bethlehem, and said to them,

"Go and inquire particularly about the child, and when you

have found him, bring me word, so that I may go and do homage to him too."

So they obeyed the king and went, and the star which they had seen rise led them on until it reached the place where I was, and stopped above it. When they saw the star, they were very glad, and they came into the house and saw me with my mother, Mary, and they threw themselves down and did homage to me. They opened their treasure boxes and presented me with gifts of gold, frankincense, and myrrh. Then, as they had been divinely warned in a dream not to go back to Herod, they returned to their own country another way.

We Flee Into Egypt

When they were gone, an angel of the Lord appeared to Joseph in a dream, and said,

"Wake up! Take the child and his mother and make your escape to Egypt, and stay there until I tell you to leave. For Herod is going to look for the child in order to make away with him."

Then Joseph awoke and took me and my mother by night and took refuge in Egypt, to fulfil what the Lord said by the prophet, "I called my son from Egypt."

Then Herod saw that he had been tricked by the astrologers, and he was very angry, and he sent and made away with all the boys in Bethlehem and in all that neighborhood who were two years old or under, for that was the time he had learned from the astrologers by his inquiries. Then the saying was fulfilled which was uttered by the prophet Jeremiah,

"A cry was heard in Ramah!
Weeping and great lamenting!
Rachel weeping for her children,
And inconsolable because they were gone."

[18]

Our Return to Nazareth

But when Herod died, an angel of the Lord appeared in a dream to Joseph, my father, in Egypt and said,

"Wake up! Take the child and his mother and go to the land of Israel, for those who sought the child's life are dead."

Then he awoke, and took me and my mother, and went to the land of Israel. But hearing that Archelaus was reigning over Judea in the place of his father, Herod, my father was afraid to return there; and being warned in a dream, he took refuge in the region of Galilee, and he went and settled in a town called Nazareth, in fulfilment of the saying of the prophets,

"He shall be called a Nazarene."

As I grew older I gained in wisdom and won the approval of God and men.

My Boyhood Visit to Jerusalem

My parents used to go to Jerusalem every year at the Passover Festival. And when I was twelve years old, we went up as usual to the festival and made the customary stay. When my parents started back I stayed behind in Jerusalem without their knowledge. They supposed that I was somewhere in the party, and traveled until the end of the first day's journey, and then they looked everywhere for me among our relatives and acquaintances. As they could not find me, they came back to Jerusalem in search of me. And on the third day they found me in the Temple, sitting among the teachers, listening to them and asking them questions, and everyone who heard me was

[19]

astonished at my intelligence and at the answers I made. When my parents saw me they were amazed, and my mother said to me,

"My child, why did you treat us like this? Here your father and I have been looking for you, and have been very anxious."

I said to them,

"How did you come to look for me? Did you not know that I must be at my Fother's house?"

But they did not understand what I told them.

THE EIGHTEEN SILENT YEARS

And I went back with them to Nazareth and obeyed them. And my mother treasured all these things up in her mind.

The Voice in the Wilderness

In the fifteenth year of the reign of the Emperor Tiberius, when Pontius Pilate was governor of Judea, and Herod governor of Galilee, a message from God came to Zechariah's son John, my cousin, in the desert.

John wore clothing made of hair cloth, and he had a leather belt around his waist, and he lived on dried locusts and wild honey.

And he went all through the Jordan Valley preaching repentance and baptism in order to obtain the forgiveness of sins, and saying, "Repent! for the Kingdom of Heaven is coming!"

It was he who was spoken of by the prophet Isaiah, when he said,

> "Hark! Someone is shouting in the desert,
> Get the Lord's way ready!

Make his paths straight!'
Every hollow must be filled up,
And every mountain and hill leveled.
What is crooked is to be made straight,
And the rough roads are to be made smooth,
And all mankind is to see how God can save!"

And all Judea and everybody in Jerusalem went out to him there, and accepted baptism from him in the Jordan River, acknowledging their sins.

But when he saw many of the Pharisees and Sadducees coming for baptism, he said to them,

"You brood of snakes! Who warned you to escape from the wrath that is coming? Then produce fruit that will be consistent with your professed repentance! Do not suppose that you can say to yourselves, 'We have Abraham for our forefather,' for I tell you God can produce descendants for Abraham right out of these stones! But the axe is already lying at the roots of the trees. Any tree that fails to produce good fruit is going to be cut down and thrown into the fire."

The crowds would ask John, "Then what ought we to do?"

And he answered,

"The man who has two shirts must share with the man who has none, and the man who has food must do the same."

Even tax-collectors came to be baptized, and they said to him,

"Master, what ought we to do?"

He said to them,

"Do not collect any more than you are authorized to."

And soldiers would ask him,

"And what ought we to do?"

He said to them,

"Do not extort money or make false charges against people, but be satisfied with your pay."

As all this aroused people's expectations, and they were all wondering in their hearts whether John was the Christ, John said to them all,

"I am only baptizing you in water, but someone is coming who is stronger than I am, whose shoes I am not fit to untie.

He will baptize you in the holy Spirit and in fire. He has his winnowing fork in his hand, to clean up his threshing-floor, and store his wheat in his barn, but he will burn up the chaff with inextinguishable fire."

So with many varied exhortations he would preach the good news to the people.

My Baptism

It was in those days that I came from Nazareth in Galilee and was baptized by John in the Jordan. But John tried to dissuade me, and said,

"I need to be baptized by you, and do you come to me?"

But I answered,

"Let it be so this time, for it is right for us to do everything that God requires."

Then John consented. And when I was baptized, I went right up out of the water, and the heavens opened, and I saw the Spirit of God come down like a dove and light upon me, and a voice from heaven said,

"This is my Son, my Beloved! This is my Chosen."

Temptation in the Wilderness

Then I was guided by the Spirit into the desert, to be tempted by the devil. And I fasted forty days and nights, and after it I was famished. And the tempter came up and said to me,

"If you are God's son, tell these stones to turn into bread!"

But I answered,

"The Scripture says, 'Not on bread alone is man to live, but on every word that comes from the mouth of God!' "

Then the devil took me to the holy city, and made me stand on the summit of the Temple, and said to me,

"If you are God's son, throw yourself down, for the Scripture says,

" 'He will give his angels orders about you,
And they will lift you up with their hands
So that you may never strike your foot against a stone!' "

I said to him,
"The Scripture also says, 'You shall not try the Lord your God.' "
Again the devil took me to a very high mountain, and he showed me all the kingdoms of the world and their splendor, and said to me,
"I will give all this to you, if you will fall on your knees and do homage to me."
Then I said to him,
"Begone, Satan! For the Scripture says, 'You must do homage to the Lord your God, and worship him alone!' "
Then the devil left me, and angels came and waited on me.

John's Testimony

Now this is the testimony that John gave when the Jews sent priests and Levites to him from Jerusalem to ask him who he was. He admitted—he made no attempt to deny it—he admitted that he was not the Christ. Then they asked him,
"What are you then? Are you Elijah?"
He said, "No, I am not."
"Are you the Prophet?"
He answered, "No."
Then they said to him, "Who are you? We must have some answer to give those who sent us here. What have you to say for yourself?"
He said, "I am a voice of one shouting in the desert, 'Straighten the Lord's way!' as the prophet Isaiah said."
Now these messengers were Pharisees. And they asked him,

[23]

"Then why are you baptizing people, if you are not the Christ, nor Elijah, nor the Prophet?"

"I am only baptizing in water," John answered, "but someone is standing among you of whom you do not know. He is to come after me, and I am not worthy to undo his shoe!"

This took place at Bethany, on the farther side of the Jordan, where John was baptizing.

The next day he saw me coming toward him, and he said,

"There is God's lamb, who is to remove the world's sin! This is the man of whom I spoke when I said, 'After me there is coming a man who is even now ahead of me, for he existed before me.' I did not know him, but it is in order that he may be made known to Israel that I have come and baptized people in water."

In the beginning I existed. I was with God, and I was divine. I was with God in the beginning. Everything came into existence through me, and apart from me nothing came to be. It was by me that life came into existence, and that life was the light of mankind. The light is still shining in the darkness, for the darkness has never put it out.

When John appeared with a message from God, he came to give testimony, to testify to the light, so that everyone might come to believe in it through him. He was not the light; he came to testify to the light.

The real light, which sheds light upon everyone, was just coming into the world. I came into the world, and though the world came into existence through me, the world did not recognize me. I came to my home, and my own family did not welcome me. But to all who did receive me and believe in me I gave the right to become children of God, owing their birth not to nature nor to any human or physical impulse, but to God.

So I became flesh and blood and lived for a while among you abounding in blessing and truth, and you saw the honor God had given me, such honor as an only son receives from his father. (John the Baptist testified to me and cried out—for it was he who said it—"He who was to come after me is now ahead of me, for he existed before me!")

And John gave this testimony:

[24]

"I saw the Spirit come down from heaven like a dove, and it remained upon him. I did not know him, but he who sent me to baptize in water said to me, 'The one on whom you see the Spirit come down and remain, is the one who is to baptize in the holy Spirit.' And I did see it, and I testify that he is the Son of God."

The First Disciples by the Jordan

Again the next day John was standing with two of his disciples, and looking at me as I passed, he said,
"There is God's lamb!"
The two disciples heard him say this, and they followed me. I turned, and seeing them following me I said,
"What do you want?"
They said to me, "Rabbi"—that is to say, Master—"Where are you staying?"
I said to them, "Come and you will see."
So they came and saw where I was staying, and they spent the rest of the day with me. It was about four in the afternoon.
Andrew, Simon Peter's brother, was one of the two who heard what John said and followed me. Andrew immediately sought out his own brother and said to him, "We have found the Messiah!"—that is to say, the Christ.
He brought him to me. I looked at him and said,
"You are Simon, son of John. You shall be called Cephas" —that is, Peter, which means rock.
The next day I was determined to leave for Galilee. And I sought out Philip and said to him,
"Come with me."
Now Philip came from Bethsaida, the town of Andrew and Peter. Philip sought out Nathanael, and said to him,
"We have found the one about whom Moses wrote in the Law and about whom the prophets wrote; it is Jesus, the son of Joseph, who comes from Nazareth!"

[25]

Nathanael said to him, "Can anything good come from Nazareth?"

Philip said to him, "Come and see!"

I saw Nathanael coming toward me, and I said of him, "Here is really an Israelite without any deceit in him!"

Nathanael said to me, "How do you know me?"

I answered, "While you were still under that fig tree, before Philip called you I saw you."

Nathanael answered, "Master, you are the Son of God! You are king of Israel!"

I answered, "Do you believe in me because I told you that I had seen you under that fig tree? You will see greater things than that!" And I said to him, "I tell you all, you will see heaven opened and God's angels going up, and coming down to the Son of Man!"

The First Miracle

Two days later there was a wedding at Cana in Galilee, and my mother was there. My disciples and I were also invited to the wedding. The wine gave out, and my mother said to me,

"They have no more wine!"

I said to her, "Do not try to direct me. It is not yet time for me to act."

My mother said to the servants, "Do whatever he tells you."

Now there were six stone water jugs there, for the ceremonial purification practiced by the Jews, each large enough to hold twenty or thirty gallons. I said to them, "Fill these jars with water."

So they filled them full. And I said to them, "Now draw some out and take it to the master of the feast."

And they did so. When the master of the feast tasted the water which had now turned into wine, without knowing where it had come from—though the servants who had drawn the water knew—he called the bridegroom and said to him,

"Everyone else serves his good wine first, and his poorer

[26]

wine after people have drunk deeply, but you have kept back your good wine till now!"

This, the first of the signs of my mission, I showed at Cana in Galilee. When my disciples saw my powers, they believed in me.

After this I went down to Capernaum with my mother, my brothers, and my disciples, and we stayed there for a few days.

Now when I was at Jerusalem, at the Passover Festival, many others when they saw the signs that I showed, came to believe in me. But I would not trust myself to them, for I knew them all, and had no need of anybody's evidence about men, for I knew well what was in their hearts.

The Visit of Nicodemus

Among the Pharisees there was a man named Nicodemus, a leader among the Jews. This man came to me one night, and said to me,

"Master, we know that you are a teacher who has come from God, for no one can show the signs that you do, unless God is with him."

I answered him, "I tell you, no one can see the Kingdom of God unless he is born over again from above!"

Nicodemus said to me, "How can a man be born when he is old? Can he enter his mother's womb over again and be born?"

I answered,

"I tell you, if a man does not owe his birth to water and spirit, he cannot get into the Kingdom of God. Whatever owes its birth to the physical is physical, and whatever owes its birth to the Spirit is spiritual. Do not wonder at my telling you that you must be born over again from above. The wind blows wherever it chooses, and you hear the sound of it, but you do not know where it comes from or where it goes. That is the way with everyone who owes his birth to the Spirit."

Nicodemus said to me, "How can that be?"

I answered,

"Are you the teacher of Israel and yet ignorant of this? I tell you we know what we are talking about and we have seen the things we testify to, yet you all reject our testimony. If you will not believe the earthly things that I have told you, how can you believe the heavenly things I have to tell? No one has yet gone up into heaven except the Son of Man who came down from heaven. And just as Moses in the desert lifted the serpent up in the air, the Son of Man must be lifted up, so that everyone who believes in him may have eternal life."

For God loved the world so much that he gave me, his only Son, so that no one who believes in me should be lost, but that they should all have eternal life. God did not send me into the world to pass judgment upon the world, but that through me the world might be saved. No one who believes in me has to come up for judgment. Anyone who does not believe stands condemned already, for not believing in God's only Son. And the basis of the judgment is this, that the light has come into the world, and yet, because their actions were wicked, men have loved the darkness more than the light. For everyone who does wrong hates the light and will not come to it, for fear his actions will be exposed. But everyone who is living the truth will come to the light, to show that his actions have been performed in dependence upon God.

PREPARATORY PREACHING

Baptizing and Preaching

After this I went into the country of Judea with my disciples, and stayed there with them and baptized—though it was not I who baptized them, but my disciples. I was about thirty years old when I began my work.

John too was baptizing at Aenon, near Salim, for there was

plenty of water there, and people came there and were baptized. For John had not yet been put in prison.

John's Tribute to Me

So a discussion arose between John's disciples and a man from Judea, about purification. And they went to John and said to him,

"Master, the man who was with you across the Jordan, and to whom you yourself gave testimony, is baptizing, and everybody is going to him."

John answered,

"A man cannot get anything unless it is given to him from heaven. You will bear me witness that I said, 'I am not the Christ; I have been sent in advance of him.' It is the bridegroom who has the bride; but the bridegroom's friend who stands outside and listens for his voice is very glad when he hears the bridegroom speak. So this happiness of mine is now complete. He must grow greater and greater, but I less and less."

At Jacob's Well

I learned that the Pharisees had been told that I was gaining and baptizing more disciples than John, so I left Judea and went back again to Galilee. Now I had to pass through Samaria. I came to a town in Samaria called Sychar, near the field that Jacob gave to his son Joseph, and Jacob's spring was there. I was tired with the journey, so I sat down by the spring. It was about noon. A woman of Samaria came to draw water. I said to her,

"Give me a drink."

For my disciples had gone into the town to buy some food.
So the Samaritan woman said to me,

"How is it that a Jew like you asks a Samaritan woman like
me for a drink? For Jews have nothing to do with Samaritans."
I answered,

"If you knew what God has to give, and who it is that said
to you, 'Give me a drink,' you would have asked him, and he
would have given you living water."

She said to me,

"You have nothing to draw water with, sir, and the well is
deep. Where can you get your living water? Are you a greater
man than our forefather Jacob, who gave us this well, and
drank from it himself, with his sons and his flocks?"

I answered,

"Anyone who drinks this water will be thirsty again, but
anyone who drinks the water that I will give him will never
be thirsty, but the water that I will give him will become a
spring of water within him, bubbling up for eternal life."

The woman said to me,

"Give me this water, sir, so that I may never be thirsty, nor
have to come all this way to draw water."

I said to her,

"Go and call your husband and come back here."

The woman answered,

"I have no husband."

I said to her,

"You are right when you say you have no husband, for you
have had five husbands and the man you are now living with
is not your husband. What you say is true."

The woman said to me,

"I see that you are a prophet, sir. Our forefathers worshiped
God on this mountain, and yet you Jews say that the place
where people must worship God is at Jerusalem."

I said to her,

"Believe me, the time is coming when you will worship the
Father neither on this mountain nor at Jerusalem. You worship something you know nothing about; we know what we
worship, for salvation comes from the Jews. But a time is
coming—it is already here!—when the true worshipers will

worship the Father in spirit and sincerity, for the Father wants such worshipers. God is spirit, and his worshipers must worship him in spirit and in sincerity."

The woman said to me,

"I know that the Messiah is coming—he who is called the Christ. When he comes, he will tell us everything!"

I said to her, "I who am talking to you am he!"

I Preach to the Samaritans

Just then my disciples came back, and they were surprised to find me talking with a woman, yet no one of them asked me what I wanted or why I was talking with her. So the woman left her pitcher and went back to the town, and said to the people,

"Come, here is a man who has told me everything I ever did! Do you suppose he is the Christ?"

The people came out of the town to see me.

Meanwhile the disciples urged me, saying, "Master, eat something."

But I said to them, "I have food to eat of which you do not know."

So the disciples said to one another,

"Do you suppose that someone has brought him something to eat?"

I said to them,

"My food is doing the will of him who has sent me, and finishing his work. Are you not saying, 'Four months more and the harvest will come'? Look, I tell you! Raise your eyes and see the fields, for they are white for harvesting. The reaper is already being paid and gathering the harvest for eternal life, so that the sower may be glad with the reaper. For here the saying holds good, 'One sows, another reaps.' I have sent you to reap a harvest on which you have not worked. Other men have worked and you have profited by their work."

[31]

Many of the Samaritans in that town came to believe in me because of the testimony the woman gave when she said, "He has told me everything I ever did!" So when the Samaritans came to me they asked me to stay with them, and I stayed there two days. And a great many more believed because of what I said, and they said to the woman,

"It is no longer because of your statement that we believe, for we have heard him ourselves, and we know that he is really the Savior of the world."

ONE YEAR OF POPULARITY

In Galilee

John the Baptist Imprisoned

Meanwhile Herod the governor had sent and seized my cousin John and bound him and put him in prison, on account of Herodias, his brother Philip's wife, because Herod had married her. John had said to Herod,

"It is not right for you to be living with your brother's wife."

Herodias felt bitterly toward John and wanted him killed. But she could not bring it about, for Herod stood in awe of John, knowing that he was an upright and holy man, and he protected him. And while he wanted him killed, he was afraid of the people, for they considered him a prophet.

My Reception by the Galileans

I returned to Galilee under the power of the Spirit. The Galileans welcomed me, for they had seen everything I had done at Jerusalem, at the festival, for they too had gone to the festival.

And news of my arrival went all over that region. I taught in the synagogues, proclaiming the good news from God, saying,

"The time has come and the reign of God is near; repent, and believe this good news."

Healing the Nobleman's Son

I came back to Cana in Galilee, where I had made the water into wine. There was at Capernaum one of the king's officials whose son was sick. When he heard that I had come back from Judea to Galilee, he came to me and begged me to come down and cure his son, for he was at the point of death. I said to him,

"Unless you see signs and marvels you will never believe!"

The official said to me, "Come down, sir, before my child is dead!"

I said to him,

"You can go home. Your son is going to live."

The man believed what I said to him and went home. While he was on the way, his slaves met him and told him that his boy was going to live. So he asked them at what time he had begun to get better, and they said to him,

"Yesterday at one o'clock the fever left him."

So the father knew that it was the very time when I had

[33]

said to him "Your son is going to live." And he and his whole household believed in me. This second sign I showed after coming back from Judea to Galilee.

The Call of Simon Peter and Andrew and James and John

As I was passing along the shore of the Sea of Galilee, I saw Simon and his brother Andrew casting their nets in the sea, for they were fishermen.

As the crowd was pressing about me to hear God's message, I was standing by the Lake of Gennesaret, and I saw two boats on the shore of the lake, for the fishermen had gotten out of them and were washing their nets. And I got into one of the boats, which belonged to Simon, and asked him to push out a little from the shore. Then I sat down and taught the crowds of people from the boat. When I stopped speaking, I said to Simon,

"Push out into deep water, and then put down your nets for a haul."

Simon answered,

"Master, we worked all night and caught nothing, but as you tell me to do it, I will put down the nets."

So they did so, and inclosed such a shoal of fish that their nets began to break. And they signaled to their comrades in the other boat to come and help them. And they came, and they filled both boats so full that they began to sink. When Simon Peter saw it, he fell down at my feet and said,

"Leave me, Master, for I am a sinful man."

For he and all the men with him were perfectly amazed at the haul of fish they had made, and so were Zebedee's sons, James and John, who were Simon's partners. I said to Simon,

"Do not be afraid. From now on you are to catch men!"

And they brought the boats to land and left everything and followed me.

[34]

A Day of Good Deeds in Capernaum

On the Sabbath I went to the synagogue and taught. And they were amazed at my teaching, for I taught them like one who had authority, and not like the scribes. There was a man in the synagogue who was possessed by the spirit of a foul demon and he cried out loudly,

"Ha! What do you want of us, Jesus, you Nazarene? Have you come to destroy us? I know who you are! You are God's holy One!"

I reproved him and said, "Silence! Get out of him!"

And the demon threw the man down in the midst of us, and came out of him, without doing him any harm. And they were all amazed and said to one another,

"What is the meaning of this teaching? For he gives orders authoritatively and effectually to the foul spirits, and they come out." And news of me spread to every place in that region.

When I got up and left the synagogue, I went to Simon's house. And Simon's mother-in-law was suffering with a severe attack of fever, and they asked me about her. And I stood over her and reproved the fever and it left her, and she got up and waited on us.

In the evening, after sunset, they brought to me all who were sick or possessed by demons, and the whole town was gathered at the door. And I cured many who were sick with various diseases, and drove out many demons, and I would not let the demons speak, because they knew that I was Christ. And I laid my hands on every one of them and cured all who were sick, in fulfilment of the words of the prophet Isaiah, "He took our sickness and carried away our diseases."

[35]

The First Leper Healed

Early in the morning, long before daylight, I got up and left the house and went off to a lonely spot, and prayed there. And Simon and his companions sought me and found me, and said to me, "They are all looking for you!"

I said to them, "Let us go somewhere else, to the neighboring country towns, so that I may preach in them, too, for that is why I came out here."

So I went all through Galilee, preaching in their synagogues and driving out the demons.

There came to me a leper appealing to me on his knees, saying to me,

"If you only choose, you can cure me."

And I pitied him and stretched out my hand and touched him, and said to him, "I do choose! Be cured!"

And the leprosy immediately left him, and he was cured. And I immediately sent him away with stern injunctions, saying to him,

"See that you say nothing about this to anybody, but begone! show yourself to the priest, and in proof of your cure make the offerings for your purification which Moses prescribed."

But he went off and began to talk so much about it, and to spread the story so widely, that I could no longer go into a town openly, but stayed out in unfrequented places, and people came to me from every direction. The power of the Lord was there, so that I might cure people.

[36]

BEGINNING OF CONTROVERSY

The Healing of a Paralytic

Some days later when I came back to Capernaum, people heard that I was at home, and such a crowd gathered that after a while there was no room even around the door, and I was telling them my message. And some people came bringing to me a man who was paralyzed, four of them carrying him. As they could not get him near me on account of the crowd, they broke open the roof just over my head, and through the opening they lowered the mat with the paralytic lying on it. When I saw their faith, I said to the paralytic,

"My son, your sins are forgiven."

There were some scribes sitting there pondering and saying to themselves,

"Why does this man talk so? This is blasphemy. Who can forgive sins but God alone?"

I at once perceived by my spirit that they were wondering over this, and said to them,

"Why do you ponder over this in your minds? Which is easier, to say to this paralytic, 'Your sins are forgiven,' or to say to him, 'Get up and pick up your mat and walk'? But to let you know that the Son of Man has authority to forgive sins on earth," I said, turning to the paralytic, "I tell you, get up, pick up your mat, and go home!"

And he got up, and immediately picked up his mat and went out before them all, so that they were all astonished and acknowledged the power of God, saying,

"We never saw anything like this before."

[37]

A Publican Disciple

I went out of the town again and along the shore of Galilee, and all the people came to me and I taught them. And as I was passing along I saw Levi, the son of Alpheus, sitting at the tollhouse, and I said to him,

"Follow me."

And he got up and followed me.

Then Levi gave a great entertainment for me in his house, and there was a great throng of tax-collectors and others who were at table with us. And the Pharisees observed it, and they said to my disciples,

"Why does your master eat with tax-collectors and irreligious people?"

But I heard it, and said,

"It is not well people but the sick who have to have the doctor! You must go and learn what the saying means, 'It is mercy, not sacrifice, that I care for.' I did not come to invite the pious but the irreligious."

The Old and the New

Now John's disciples and the Pharisees were keeping a fast. And people came and asked me,

"John's disciples observe frequent fasts and offer prayers, and so do the disciples of the Pharisees, but your disciples eat and drink."

I said to them,

"Can you make wedding guests fast while the bridegroom is with them? But other days will come, and when the bridegroom is taken away from them, in those days they will fast."

I used this figure also in speaking to them:

"No one tears a piece from a new coat and sews it on an old one, or if he does, he will both tear the new one and the piece from the new one will not match the old one. And nobody puts new wine into old wine-skins, or if he does, the new wine will burst the skins and run out, and the skins will be spoiled. New wine has to be put into fresh skins. No one after drinking old wine wants new, for he says, 'The old is better!' "

A Sabbath Healing in Jerusalem

After this there was a festival of the Jews, and I went up to Jerusalem. Now there is in Jerusalem near the Sheepgate a pool called in Hebrew Bethzatha, which has five colonnades. In these there used to lie a great number of people who were sick, blind, lame, or paralyzed. There was one man there who had been sick for thirty-eight years. I saw him lying there, and finding that he had been in this condition for a long time, said to him,

"Do you want to get well?"

The sick man answered,

"I have nobody, sir, to put me into the pool when the water stirs, but while I am getting down someone else steps in ahead of me."

I said to him,

"Get up, pick up your mat, and walk!"

And the man was immediately cured, and he picked up his mat and walked.

Now it was the Sabbath. So the Jews said to the man who had been cured,

"It is the Sabbath, and it is against the Law for you to carry your mat."

But he answered,

"The man who cured me said to me, 'Pick up your mat and walk.' "

They asked him,

"Who was it that said to you, 'Pick it up and walk'?"

But the man who had been cured did not know who it was, for as there was a crowd there, I had left the place. Afterward I found him in the Temple, and said to him,

"See! You are well again. Give up sin, or something worse may happen to you."

The man went and told the Jews that it was I who had cured him. This was why the Jews used to persecute me, because I did things like this on the Sabbath. But I answered them,

"My Father is still at work, and I work too."

On account of this the Jews were all the more eager to kill me, because I not only broke the Sabbath but actually called God my Father, thus putting myself on an equality with God. So I answered them,

"I tell you, the Son cannot do anything of his own accord, unless he sees the Father doing it. For whatever the Father does, the Son also does. For the Father loves the Son and lets him see everything that he himself is doing, and he will let him see greater deeds than these, to make you wonder. For just as the Father awakens the dead and makes them come to life, the Son makes anyone whom he chooses come to life. For the Father passes judgment on no one, but he has committed the judgment entirely to the Son, so that all men may honor the Son just as much as they honor the Father. Whoever refuses to honor the Son refuses to honor the Father who sent him. I tell you, whoever listens to my message and believes him who has sent me, possesses eternal life, and will not come to judgment, but has already passed out of death into life. I tell you, the time is coming—it is here already!— when those who are dead will listen to the voice of the Son of God, and those who listen to it will live. For just as the Father is self-existent, he has given self-existence to the Son, and he has given him the authority to act as judge, because he is a son of man. Do not be surprised at this, for the time is coming when all who are in their graves will listen to his voice, and those who have done right will come out to resurrection and life, and those who have done wrong, to resurrection and judgment. I cannot do anything of my own accord.

I pass judgment just as I am told to do, and my judgment is just, for I am not seeking to do what I please but what pleases him who has sent me.

"I do not testify to myself. It is someone else who testifies to me, and I know that the testimony that he gives about me is true. You yourselves sent to John, and he testified to the truth. But the testimony that I accept is not from any man; I am only saying this that you may be saved. He was the lamp that burned and shone, and you were ready to be gladdened for a while by his light. But I have higher testimony than John's, for the things that my Father has intrusted to me to accomplish, the very things that I am doing, are proof that my Father has sent me, and my Father who has sent me has thus borne witness to me. You have never heard his voice or seen his form, and you do not keep his message in your hearts, for you do not believe the messenger whom he has sent. You pore over the Scriptures, for you think that you will find eternal life in them, and these very Scriptures testify to me, yet you refuse to come to me for life. I do not accept any honor from men, but I know well that you have not the love of God in your hearts. I have come in my Father's name, and you refuse to accept me. If someone else comes in his own name you will accept him. Yet how can you believe in me, when you accept honor from one another, instead of seeking the honor that comes from the one God?

Do not suppose that I will accuse you to the Father. Moses is your accuser—Moses, on whom you have fixed your hopes! For if you really believed Moses, you would believe me, for it was about me that he wrote. But if you refuse to believe what he wrote, how are you ever to believe what I say?"

Plucking Grain on the Sabbath

At that same time I walked one Sabbath through the wheat fields, and my disciples became hungry and began to pick the heads of wheat and eat them. But the Pharisees saw it and said to me,

[41]

"Look! Your disciples are doing something which it is against the Law to do on the Sabbath!"

But I said to them,

"Did you never read what David did, when he and his companions were hungry? How is it that he went into the House of God and that they ate the Presentation Loaves which it was against the Law for him and his companions to eat, or for anyone except the priests? Or did you never read in the Law how the priests in the Temple are not guilty when they break the Sabbath? But I tell you, there is something greater than the Temple here! But if you knew what the saying means, 'It is mercy, not sacrifice, that I care for,' you would not have condemned men who are not guilty.

"The Sabbath was made for man, not man for the Sabbath, and so the Son of Man is master even of the Sabbath."

Many Called and Few Chosen

Word went all through Syria about me, and people brought to me all who were suffering with any kind of disease, or who were in great pain—demoniacs, epileptics, and paralytics—and I cured them.

So I retired with my disciples to the seashore, and a great many people from Galilee followed me, and from Judea and Jerusalem and Idumea and from the other side of the Jordan and from the neighborhood of Tyre and Sidon a great many who had heard of the things I was doing came to me. I told my disciples to have a boat always ready for my use, to prevent my being crushed by the crowd. For I cured so many people that all who had any ailments pressed up to me to touch me. And whenever the foul spirits saw me, they fell down before me and screamed out,

"You are the Son of God!" And I warned them repeatedly not to tell who I was, in fulfilment of what was said by the prophet Isaiah,

[42]

" 'Here is my servant whom I have selected,
My beloved, who delights my heart!
I will endow him with my Spirit,
And he will announce a judgment to the heathen.
He will not wrangle or make an outcry,
And no one will hear his voice in the streets;
He will not break off a bent reed,
And he will not put out a smoldering wick,
Until he carries his judgment to success.
The heathen will rest their hopes on his name.' "

Selection of the Twelve

In those days I went up on the mountain to pray, and passed the whole night in prayer to God. When day came, I called my disciples to me, and chose twelve of them whom I named apostles, to be with me and to be sent out to preach, with power to drive out the demons. These were the twelve I appointed: Peter, which was the name I gave to Simon, James the son of Zebedee, and John, James's brother (I named them Boanerges, that is, Sons of Thunder), Andrew, Philip, Bartholomew, Matthew, Thomas, James the son of Alpheus, Thaddeus, Simon the Zealot, and Judas Iscariot, who later betrayed me.

THE TEACHING OF THE KINGDOM

The Citizens of the Kingdom

When I saw the crowds of people I went up on the mountain.
There I seated myself, and when my disciples had come up
to me, I opened my lips to teach them. And I said,

"Blessed are those who feel their spiritual need, for the
Kingdom of Heaven belongs to them!

"Blessed are the mourners, for they will be consoled!

"Blessed are the humble-minded, for they will possess the
land!

"Blessed are those who are hungry and thirsty for uprightness, for they will be satisfied!

"Blessed are the merciful, for they will be shown mercy!

"Blessed are the pure in heart, for they will see God!

"Blessed are the peacemakers, for they will be called God's
sons!

"Blessed are those who have endured persecution for their
uprightness, for the Kingdom of Heaven belongs to them!

"Blessed are you when people abuse you, and persecute
you, and falsely say everything bad of you, on my account.
Be glad and exult over it, for you will be richly rewarded in
heaven, for that is the way they persecuted the prophets who
went before you!

"You are the salt of the earth! But if salt loses its strength,
how can it be made salt again? It is good for nothing but to
be thrown away and trodden underfoot. You are the light of
the world! A city that is built upon a hill cannot be hidden.
People do not light a lamp and put it under a peck-measure;
they put it on its stand and it gives light to everyone in the
house. Your light must burn in that way among men so that

they will <u>see the good</u> you do, and praise your Father in heaven.

The Righteousness of the Kingdom

"Do not suppose that I have come to do away with the Law or the Prophets. I have not come to do away with them but to enforce them. For I tell you, as long as heaven and earth endure, not one dotting of an *i* or crossing of a *t* will be dropped from the Law until it is all observed. Anyone, therefore, who weakens one of the slightest of these commands, and teaches others to do so, will be ranked lowest in the Kingdom of Heaven; but anyone who observes them and teaches others to do so will be ranked high in the Kingdom of Heaven. For I tell you that unless your uprightness is far superior to that of the scribes and Pharisees, you will never even enter the Kingdom of Heaven!

"You have heard that the men of old were told, 'You shall not murder,' and 'Whoever murders will have to answer to the court.' But I tell you that anyone who gets angry with his brother will have to answer to the court, and anyone who speaks contemptuously to his brother will have to answer to the great council, and anyone who says to his brother, 'You cursed fool!' will have to answer for it in the fiery pit! So when you are presenting your gift at the altar, if you remember that your brother has any grievance against you, leave your gift right there before the altar and go and make up with your brother; then come back and present your gift. Be quick and come to terms with your opponent while you are on the way to court with him, or he may hand you over to the judge, and the judge may hand you over to the officer, and you will be thrown into prison. I tell you, you will never get out again until you have paid the last penny!

"You have heard that men were told, 'You shall not commit adultery.' But I tell you that anyone who looks at a woman with desire has already committed adultery with her in his heart. But if your right eye makes you fall, tear it out and throw it away, for you might better lose one part of your body than have it all thrown into the pit! If your right hand makes you fall, cut it off and throw it away, for you might better lose one part of your body than have it all go down to the pit!

"They were told, 'Anyone who divorces his wife must give her a certificate of divorce.' But I tell you that anyone who divorces his wife on any ground, except unfaithfulness, makes her commit adultery, and anyone who marries her after she is divorced commits adultery.

"Again, you have heard that the men of old were told, 'You shall not swear falsely, but you must fulfil your oaths to the Lord.' But I tell you not to swear at all, either by heaven, for it is God's throne, or by the earth, for it is his footstool, or by Jerusalem, for it is the city of the great king. You must not swear by your own head, for you cannot make one single hair white or black. But your way of speaking must be 'Yes' or 'No.' Anything that goes beyond that comes from the evil one.

"You have heard that they were told, 'An eye for an eye and a tooth for a tooth.' But I tell you not to resist injury, but if anyone strikes you on your right cheek, turn the other to him too; and if anyone wants to sue you for your shirt, let him have your coat too. And if anyone forces you to go one mile, go two miles with him. If anyone begs from you, give to him, and when anyone wants to borrow from you, do not turn away.

"You have heard that they were told, 'You must love your neighbor and hate your enemy.' But I tell you, love your enemies and pray for your persecutors, so that you may show yourselves true sons of your Father in heaven, for he makes his sun rise on bad and good alike, and makes the rain fall on the upright and the wrongdoers. For if you love only those who love you, what reward can you expect? Do not the very tax-collectors do that? And if you are polite to your brothers and no one else, what is there remarkable in that? Do not the very heathen do that? So you are to be perfect, as your heavenly Father is.

[46]

The Danger of Hypocrisy

"But take care not to do your good deeds in public for people to see, for, if you do, you will get no reward from your Father in heaven. So when you are going to give to charity, do not blow a trumpet before yourself, as the hypocrites do, in the synagogues and the streets, to make people praise them. I tell you, that is all the reward they will get! But when you give to charity, your own left hand must not know what your right hand is doing, so that your charity may be secret, and your Father who sees what is secret will reward you.

"When you pray, you must not be like the hypocrites, for they like to pray standing in the synagogues and in the corners of the squares, to let people see them. I tell you, that is the only reward they will get! But when you pray, go into your own room, and shut the door, and pray to your Father who is unseen, and your Father who sees what is secret will reward you. And when you pray, do not repeat empty phrases as the heathen do, for they imagine that their prayers will be heard if they use words enough. You must not be like them. For God, who is your Father, knows what you need before you ask him. This, therefore, is the way you are to pray:

'Our Father in heaven,
Your name be revered!
Your kingdom come!
Your will be done on earth as it is done in heaven!
Give us today bread for the day,
And forgive us our debts, as we have forgiven our
  debtors.
And do not subject us to temptation,
But save us from the evil one.'

For if you forgive others when they offend you, your heavenly Father will forgive you too. But if you do not forgive others when they offend you, your heavenly Father will not forgive you for your offenses.

"When you fast, do not put on a gloomy look, like the hypocrites, for they neglect their personal appearance to let people see that they are fasting. I tell you, that is all the reward they will get. But when you fast, perfume your hair and wash your face, so that no one may see that you are fasting, except your Father who is unseen, and your Father who sees what is secret, will reward you.

Simple Trust in God

"Do not store up your riches on earth, where moths and rust destroy them, and where thieves break in and steal them, but store up your riches in heaven, where moths and rust cannot destroy them, and where thieves cannot break in and steal them. For wherever your treasure is, your heart will be also. The eye is the lamp of the body. If then your eye is sound, your whole body will be light, but if your eye is unsound, your whole body will be dark. If, therefore, your very light is darkness, how deep the darkness will be!

"No slave can belong to two masters, for he will either hate one and love the other, or stand by one and make light of the other. You cannot serve God and money. Therefore, I tell you, do not worry about life, wondering what you will have to eat or drink, or about your body, wondering what you will have to wear. Is not life more important than food, and the body than clothes? Look at the wild birds. They do not sow or reap, or store their food in barns, and yet your heavenly Father feeds them. Are you not of more account than they? But which of you with all his worry can add a single hour to his life? Why should you worry about clothing? See how the wild flowers grow. They do not toil or spin, and yet I tell you, even Solomon in all his splendor was never dressed like one of them. But if God so beautifully dresses the wild grass, which is alive today and is thrown into the furnace tomorrow, will he not much more surely clothe you, you who have so little faith? So do not worry and say, 'What shall we have to eat?' or 'What shall we have to drink?' or 'What shall we have to wear?' For these are all things the heathen are in pursuit of, and your heavenly Father knows well that you need all this. But you must make his kingdom, and uprightness before him, your greatest care, and you will have all these other things besides. So do not worry about tomorrow, for tomorrow will have worries of its own. Let each day be content with its own ills.

Charitable Judgment

"You must be merciful, just as your Father is. Do not judge others, and they will not judge you. Do not condemn them, and they will not condemn you. Excuse others and they will excuse you. Give, and they will give to you; good measure, pressed down, shaken together, and running over, they will pour into your lap. For the measure you use with others they in turn will use with you."

And I used this figure, saying,

"Can one blind man lead another? Will they not both fall into a hole? A pupil is not better than his teacher, but every pupil when he is fully trained will be like his teacher. Why do you keep looking at the speck in your brother's eye, and pay no attention to the beam that is in your own? How can you say to your brother, 'Brother, just let me get that speck out of your eye,' when you cannot see the beam in your own eye? You hypocrite! First get the beam out of your own eye, and then you can see to get out the speck in your brother's eye.

"Do not give what is sacred to dogs, and do not throw your pearls before pigs, or they will trample them under their feet and turn and tear you in pieces."

[49]

Prayer

And I said to them,

"Suppose one of you has a friend, and goes to him in the middle of the night, and says to him, 'Friend, lend me three loaves, for a friend of mine has just come to my house after a journey, and I have nothing for him to eat,' and he answers from inside, 'Do not bother me; the door is now fastened, and my children and I have gone to bed; I cannot get up and give you any.' I tell you, even if he will not get up and give him some because he is his friend, yet because of his persistence he will rouse himself and give him all he needs. So I tell you, ask, and what you ask will be given you. Search, and you will find what you search for. Knock, and the door will open to you. For it is always the one who asks who receives, and the one who searches who finds, and the one who knocks to whom the door opens. Which of you fathers, if his son asks him for a fish will give him a snake instead? Or if he asks for an egg, will give him a scorpion? So if you, bad as you are, know enough to give your children what is good, how much more surely will your Father in heaven give the holy Spirit to those who ask him for it!

Sincerity

"Go in at the narrow gate. For the road that leads to destruction is broad and spacious, and there are many who go in by it. But the gate is narrow and the road is hard that leads to life, and there are few that find it.

"Beware of the false prophets, who come to you disguised as sheep but are ravenous wolves underneath. You can tell them by their fruit. Do people pick grapes off thorns, or figs

[50]

off thistles? Just so any sound tree bears good fruit, but a poor tree bears bad fruit. No sound tree can bear bad fruit, and no poor tree can bear good fruit. Any tree that does not bear good fruit is cut down and burned. So you can tell them by their fruit.

"A good man, out of the good he has accumulated in his heart, produces good, and a bad man, out of what he has accumulated that is bad, produces what is bad. For his mouth says only what his heart is full of.

"It is not everyone who says to me 'Lord! Lord!' who will get into the Kingdom of Heaven, but only those who do the will of my Father in heaven. Many will say to me on that Day, 'Lord! Lord! was it not in your name that we prophesied, and by your name that we drove out demons, and by your name that we did many mighty acts?' Then I will say to them plainly, 'I never knew you! Go away from me, you who do wrong!'

"Everyone, therefore, who listens to this teaching of mine and acts upon it, will be like a sensible man who built his house on rock. And the rain fell, and the rivers rose, and the winds blew, and beat about that house, and it did not go down, for its foundations were on rock. And anyone who listens to this teaching of mine and does not act upon it, will be like a foolish man who built his house on sand. And the rain fell and the rivers rose, and the winds blew and beat about that house, and it went down, and its downfall was complete."

When I had finished this discourse, the crowds were astounded at my teaching, for I taught them like one who had authority and not like their scribes.

A TOUR IN GALILEE

The Worthy Centurion

When I had finished saying all this in the hearing of the people, I went to Capernaum.

A Roman captain had a slave whom he thought a great deal of, and the slave was sick and at the point of death. When the captain heard about me, he sent some Jewish elders to me, to ask me to come and save his slave's life. And they came to me and urged me strongly to do it, and said,

"He deserves to have you do this for him, for he loves our nation, and it was he who built us our synagogue."

So I went with them. But when I was not far from the house, the captain sent some friends to me, to say to me,

"Master, do not take any more trouble, for I am not a suitable person to have you under my roof. That is why I did not think I was fit to come to you. But simply say the word, and have my servant cured. For I have soldiers under me, and I tell one to go, and he goes, and another to come, and he comes, and my slave to do something, and he does it."

When I heard this, I was astonished at him, and turning to the crowd that was following me, I said,

"I tell you, I have not found such faith as this even in Israel! And I tell you, many will come from the east and from the west and take their places at the feast with Abraham, Isaac, and Jacob, in the Kingdom of Heaven, while the heirs to the kingdom will be driven into the darkness outside, there to weep and grind their teeth!"

And when the messengers went back to the house, they found the slave well.

[52]

Raising the Widow's Son

Soon afterward I happened to go to the town of Nain, and my disciples and a great throng of people were with me. As I came up to the gate of the town, a dead man was being carried out; he was his mother's only son, and she was a widow. A crowd of the townspeople was with her. And when I saw her, I pitied her, and said to her,

"Do not weep."

And I went up and touched the bier, and the bearers stopped. And I said,

"Young man, I tell you, wake up!"

And the dead man sat up and began to speak, and I gave him back to his mother. And they were all overcome with awe, and they praised God, and said,

"A great prophet has appeared among us!" and "God has not forgotten his people!"

The news about this spread all over Judea and the surrounding country.

A Question from John the Baptist

John's disciples told him in the prison of all this, and he called two of them to him, and sent them to me to ask me,

"Are you the one who was to come, or should we look for someone else?"

And the men came to me and said,

"John the Baptist sent us to you to ask, 'Are you the one who was to come, or should we look for someone else?' "

Just then I cured many of diseases and ailments and evil spirits, and I gave sight to many who were blind. And I answered them,

[53]

"Go and report to John what you have seen and heard. The blind are regaining their sight, the lame can walk, the lepers are being cured and the deaf can hear, the dead are being raised and good news is being preached to the poor. And blessed is the man who finds nothing that repels him in me."

My Estimate of John the Baptist

When John's messengers were gone, I began to speak to the crowds about John.

"What was it that you went out into the desert to look at? A reed swaying in the wind? Then what did you go out there to see? A man luxuriously dressed? Men who wear fine clothes and live in luxury you find in palaces. Then what did you go out there to see? A prophet? Yes, I tell you, and far more than a prophet! This is the man of whom the Scripture says,

" 'Here I send my messenger on before you,
He will prepare the road ahead of you!'

"I tell you, among men born of women there is none greater than John; and yet those who are of little importance in the Kingdom of God are greater than he. And all the people, even the tax-collectors, when they heard him, acknowledged the justice of God's demands, by accepting baptism from John, but the Pharisees and experts in the Law thwarted God's purpose for themselves, by refusing to be baptized by him. But from the time of John the Baptist until now men have been taking the Kingdom of Heaven by storm and impetuously crowding into it. For up to the time of John all the Prophets and the Law itself prophesied about it, and, if you are ready to accept the idea, he is himself Elijah who was to come. Let him who has ears listen! But to what can I compare this present age? It is like children sitting about in the bazaars and calling out to their playmates,

" 'We have played the flute for you, and you would not dance!

We have wailed and you would not beat your breasts!'

For when John came, he neither ate nor drank, and people said, 'He has a demon!' Now that the Son of Man has come, he does eat and drink, and people say, 'Look at him! A glutton and a drinker, the companion of tax-collectors and irreligious people!' And yet Wisdom is vindicated by her actions!"

The Death of John the Baptist

When a holiday came and Herod on his birthday gave a banquet to his courtiers and officers and to the leading men of Galilee, Herodias' own daughter came in and danced for them. And Herod and his guests were delighted, and the king said to the girl,

"Ask me for anything you like and I will give it to you." And he made oath to her,

"I will give you whatever you ask me for, up to half my kingdom."

When she had left the room she said to her mother,

"What shall I ask him for?"

But she said,

"The head of John the baptizer."

And she hurried back at once to the king and asked him for it, saying,

"I want you right away to give me John the Baptist's head on a platter."

The king was exceedingly sorry, but on account of his oath and his guests he did not like to break his word to her, and he immediately sent one of his guard with orders to get John's head. And he went off and beheaded him in the prison and brought back his head on a platter and gave it to the girl, and the girl gave it to her mother. When his disciples heard of it

[55]

they came and took his body away and put it in a tomb. Then they came and reported it to me.

Forgiveness of the Repentant Man

One of the Pharisees asked me to have dinner with him, and I went to the Pharisee's house and took my place at the table. Now there was a woman in the town who was leading a sinful life, and when she learned that I was having dinner at the Pharisee's house, she got an alabaster flask of perfume, and came and stood behind me at my feet, weeping, and began to wet my feet with her tears, and she wiped them with her hair, and kissed them, and put the perfume on them. When the Pharisee who had invited me saw this, he said to himself,

"If this man were really a prophet, he would know who and what the woman is who is touching him, for she leads a wicked life."

I said to him,

"Simon, there is something I want to say to you."

He said,

"Proceed, Master."

"Two men were in debt to a money-lender. One owed him a hundred dollars and the other ten. As they could not pay him, he canceled what they owed him. Now which of them will be more attached to him?"

Simon answered,

"The one, I suppose, for whom he canceled most."

"You are right," I said. And turning to the woman, I said to Simon,

"Do you see this woman? I came to your house; you did not give me any water for my feet, but she has wet my feet with tears and wiped them with her hair. You did not give me a kiss, but from the moment I came in she has not stopped kissing my feet. You did not put any oil upon my head, but she has put perfume upon my feet. Therefore, I tell you, her sins, many as they are, are forgiven, for she has loved me so much. But the man with little to be forgiven loves me but little."

And I said to her,

"Your sins are forgiven!"

The men at table with me began to say to themselves, "Who is this man, who even forgives sins?"

But I said to the woman,

"It is your faith that has saved you. Go in peace."

The Ministering Women

Soon afterward I went about among the villages and towns preaching and telling the good news of the Kingdom of God. The Twelve went with me, and some women who had been cured of evil spirits and sickness—Mary, who was called Mary of Magdala, out of whom seven demons had been driven, and Joanna, the wife of Chuza, Herod's manager, and Susanna, and many others, who provided for us with their means.

GROWING POPULARITY
AND RISING OPPOSITION

The Concern of My Friends

And the word came to me, "Your mother and your brothers are standing outside; they want to see you."

But I said to the man who told me,

"Who is my mother, and who are my brothers?"

And I pointed to my disciples and said,

"Here are my mother and my brothers! For whoever does

[57]

the will of my Father in heaven is my brother and sister and
mother!"

Warning of Eternal Sin

At that time some people brought to me a man blind and
dumb, who was possessed by a demon, and I cured him, so
that the dumb man could speak and see. And all the crowds
of people were astounded, and said,
"Can this be the Son of David?"
But when the Pharisees heard of it they said,
"This man cannot drive out demons except by the aid of
Beelzebub, the prince of the demons."
But I knew what they were thinking, and I said to them,
"Any kingdom that is disunited is on the way to destruction,
and any city or household that is disunited cannot last. If
Satan is driving Satan out, he is disunited, and so how can
his kingdom last? And if I am driving the demons out by
Beelzebub's aid, by whose aid do your sons drive them out?
Therefore let them be your judges. But if I am driving the
demons out by the aid of God's Spirit, then the Kingdom of
God has overtaken you. Therefore, they shall be your judges.
But if it is with the finger of God that I am driving the demons out, then the Kingdom of God has overtaken you. When
a strong man fully armed guards his own dwelling, his property is undisturbed. But when somebody stronger than he
attacks him and overcomes him, he strips him of the arms
that he relied on, and divides up the spoils. Anyone who is
not with me is against me, and anyone who does not join me
in gathering, scatters.
"I tell you, men will be forgiven for everything, for all their
sins and all the abusive things they say. But whoever reviles
the holy Spirit can never be forgiven, but is guilty of an un-
ending sin."
This was because they said, "He is possessed by a foul
spirit."

I also said to them: You brood of snakes! how can you, bad as you are, utter anything good? For the mouth says only what the heart is full of. A good man, out of the good he has accumulated, brings out things that are good, and a bad man, out of what he has accumulated that is bad, brings out things that are bad. But I tell you, for every careless word that men utter they will have to answer on the Day of Judgment. For it is by your words that you will be acquitted, or by your words that you will be condemned."

The Demand for a Sign

Then some of the scribes and Pharisees addressed me, saying,

"Master, we would like to have you show us some sign."

But I answered,

"Only a wicked and faithless age insists upon a sign, and no sign will be given it but the sign of the prophet Jonah. For just as Jonah became a sign to the people of Nineveh, so the Son of Man will be a sign to this age. The queen of the south will rise with the men of this generation at the Judgment and will condemn them, for she came from the very ends of the earth to listen to Solomon's wisdom, and there is more than Solomon here! Men of Nineveh will rise with this generation at the Judgment and will condemn it, for they repented at Jonah's preaching, and there is more than Jonah here.

"When a foul spirit goes out of a man, it roams through deserts in search of rest and can find none. Then it says, 'I will go back to my house that I left,' and it goes and finds it unoccupied, cleaned, and all in order. Then it goes and gets seven other spirits more wicked than itself, and they go in and live there, and in the end the man is worse off than he was before. That is the way it will be with this present wicked age."

As I said this, a woman in the crowd raised her voice and said to me,

"Blessed is the mother who bore you and nursed you!"

But I said,

"You might better say, 'Blessed are those who hear God's message and observe it!' "

THE PARABLES OF THE KINGDOM

The Sower

That same day I went out of my house and was sitting on the seashore. And such great crowds gathered about me that I got into a boat and sat down in it, while all the people stood on the shore. And I told them many things in figures, and said to them,

"A sower went out to sow, and as he was sowing, some of the seed fell by the path and the birds came and ate it up, and some fell on rocky ground where there was not much soil and it sprang up at once, because the soil was not deep, but when the sun came up it was scorched and withered up, because it had no root. And some of it fell among the thorns, and the thorns grew up and choked it out. And some fell on good soil, and yielded some a hundred, some sixty, and some thirty-fold. Let him who has ears listen!"

When I was by myself, those who stayed about me with the Twelve asked me about the figures I had used.

I answered,

"You are permitted to know the secrets of the Kingdom of Heaven, but they are not. For people who have will have more given to them, and will be plentifully supplied, and from people who have nothing even what they have will be taken away. This is why I speak to them in figures, because though they look they do not see, and though they listen they do not hear or understand. They are a fulfilment of Isaiah's prophecy,

" 'You will listen and listen, and never understand,
And you will look and look, and never see!
For this nation's mind has grown dull,
And they hear faintly with their ears,
And they have shut their eyes,
So as never to see with their eyes,
And hear with their ears,
And understand with their minds, and turn back,
And let me cure them!'

But blessed are your eyes, for they do see, and your ears, for they do hear. For I tell you, many prophets and upright men have longed to see what you see, and could not see it, and to hear what you hear, and could not hear it."

And I said,

"If you do not understand this figure, then how will you understand my other figures? What the sower sows is the message. The ones by the path are those into whose hearts the message falls, and as soon as they hear it Satan comes and carries off the message that has been sown in their hearts. It is so too with the ones sown on the rocky ground; they gladly accept the message as soon as they hear it, but it takes no real root in them and they last only a little while; then when trouble or persecution comes because of the message they give it up at once. It is different with those sown among the thorns. They are people who listen to the message, but the worries of the time and the pleasure of being rich and passions for other things creep in and choke the message out and it yields nothing. And the ones sown in good ground are the people who listen to the message and welcome it and yield thirty, sixty, even a hundredfold."

The Tares

Another figure which I used in speaking to them was this: "The Kingdom of Heaven is like a man who sowed good seed in his field, but while people were asleep his enemy came and sowed weeds among the wheat, and went away. And when the wheat came up and ripened, the weeds appeared too. And the owner's slaves came to him and said, 'Was not the seed good that you sowed in your field, sir? So where did these weeds come from?' He said to them, 'This is some enemy's doing.' And they said to him, 'Do you want us to go and gather them up?' But he said, 'No, for in gathering up the weeds you may uproot the wheat. Let them both grow together until harvest time, and when we harvest I will direct the reapers to gather up the weeds first and tie them up in bundles to burn, but get the wheat into my barn.'

The Growing Grain

"The reign of God," I said, "is like a man scattering seed on the ground, and then sleeping at night and getting up by day, while the seed sprouts and comes up, without his knowing it. The ground of itself is productive, putting forth first a blade, then a head, then fully developed wheat in the head. But as soon as the crop will let him, the man goes in with his sickle, for the harvest time has come.

The Mustard Seed

"How can we find any comparison," I said, "for the reign
of God, or what figure can we use to describe it? It is like a
mustard seed, which, when sown in the ground, though it is
the smallest of all the seeds in the world, yet once sown, comes
up and grows to be the largest of all the plants, and produces
branches so large that the wild birds can roost under the
shelter of it."

The Leaven

Another figure which I used with them was this:
"The Kingdom of Heaven is like yeast, which a woman
took and buried in a bushel of flour until it had all risen."

The Understanding of Parables

I said all this to the crowds in figures, and told them nothing except in figures, to fulfil what was said by the prophet,

"I will open my mouth in figures,
  I will utter things that have been hidden since the crea-
    tion."

Then I left the crowds and went into my house. And my
disciples came up to me and said,
"Explain to us the figure of the weeds in the field."
I answered,

"The sower who sows the good seed is the Son of Man. The field is the world. The good seed is the people of the kingdom. The weeds are the wicked. The enemy who sowed them is the devil. The harvest is the close of the age, and the reapers are angels. So just as the weeds are gathered up and burned, this is what will happen at the close of the age; the Son of Man will send out his angels, and they will gather up out of his kingdom all the causes of sin and the wrongdoers and throw them into the blazing furnace; there they will wail and grind their teeth. Then the upright will shine out like the sun, in their Father's kingdom. Let him who has ears listen!"

The Hid Treasure

I also told them:
"The Kingdom of Heaven is like a hoard of money, buried in a field, which a man found, and buried again. And he was overjoyed, and went and sold everything he had and bought the field.

The Pearl of Great Price

"Again the Kingdom of Heaven is like a dealer in search of fine pearls. He found one costly pearl, and went and sold everything he had, and bought it.

The Dragnet

"Again, the Kingdom of Heaven is like a net that was let down into the sea, and inclosed fish of all kinds. When it was full, they dragged it up on the beach, and sat down and sorted the good fish into baskets and threw the bad away. That is what will happen at the close of the age. The angels will go out and remove the wicked from among the upright, and throw them into the blazing furnace. There they will wail and grind their teeth.

"Do you understand all this?"

They said to me, "Yes,"

I said to them,

"Then remember this, that every scribe who becomes a disciple of the Kingdom of Heaven must be like a householder who can supply from his storeroom new things as well as old."

A DAY OF MIRACLES BY THE LAKE

I Still the Storm

That same day when it was evening I said to them,

"Let us cross to the other side."

So they left the crowd and took me away in the boat in which I was sitting. There were other boats with me. And a heavy squall of wind came on and the waves dashed into the boat, so that it was beginning to fill. I was in the stern, asleep on the cushion. And they woke me up and said to me,

"Master, does it make no difference to you that we are sinking?"

Then I awoke and reproved the wind, and said to the sea, "Hush! Silence!"

And the wind went down and there was a great calm. And I said to them,

"Why are you afraid? Have you still no faith?"

And they were very much frightened, and said to one another,

"Who can he be? For even the wind and the sea obey him."

The Legion of Demons

We made a landing in the neighborhood of Gerasa, which is just across the lake from Galilee. And when we landed, we met a man possessed by demons, who was coming out of the town. He had worn no clothing for a long time, and did not live in a house but in the tombs. When he saw me he cried out and threw himself down before me, and said in a loud voice,

"What do you want of me, Jesus, Son of the Most High God? I beg you not to torture me!"

For I was commanding the foul spirit to get out of the man. For it had often seized him, and though he had been fastened with chains and fetters, and was closely watched, he would snap his bonds and the demon would drive him away to the desert. And I asked him,

"What is your name?"

He said,

"Legion!" For many demons had gone into him. And they begged me not to order them off to the bottomless pit. Now there was a large drove of pigs feeding there on the hillside, and they begged me to give them leave to go into them. And I did so. Then the demons came out of the man and went into the pigs, and the drove of about two thousand rushed over the steep bank into the sea and were drowned. And the men who tended them ran away and spread the news in the town and in the country around, and the people came to see what had happened. When they came to me and found the demoniac sitting quietly with his clothes on and in his right mind—the same man who had been possessed by Legion—they were frightened. And those who had seen it told them what had happened to the demoniac, and all about the pigs. And they began to beg me to leave their district. As I was getting into the boat, the man who had been possessed begged to be allowed to go with me. I would not permit it, but said to him,

[66]

"Go home to your own people, and tell them all the Lord has done for you and how he took pity on you." And he went off and began to tell everybody in the Ten Towns all I had done for him; and they were all astonished.

When I had crossed again in the boat to the other side, a great crowd gathered about me as I stood on the shore. And a man named Jairus, the leader of a synagogue, came up and seeing me threw himself at my feet and appealed to me, saying,

"My little daughter is at the point of death. Come, lay your hands on her, so that she may get well and live!"

So I went with him. And a great crowd followed me and pressed around me. And a woman who had had a hemorrhage for twelve years and had had a great deal of treatment from various doctors and had spent all that she had and had not been benefited at all but had actually grown worse, had heard about me. And she came up in the crowd behind me and touched my coat, for she said,

"If I can only touch his clothes, I shall get well."

The hemorrhage stopped at once, and she felt in her body that she was cured. I instantly perceived that healing power had passed from me, and I turned around in the crowd and said,

"Who touched my clothes?"

My disciples said to me,

"You see the crowd pressing around you, and yet you ask, 'Who touched me?'"

But I still looked around to see the person who had done it. The woman, knowing what had happened to her, came forward frightened and trembling, and threw herself down at my feet and told me the whole truth. And I said to her,

"My daughter, it is your faith that has cured you. Go in peace and be free from your disease."

Even as I spoke people came from the house of the leader of the synagogue and said,

"Your daughter is dead. Why should you trouble the Master any further?"

But I paid no attention to what they said, but said to the leader of the synagogue,

"Do not be afraid, just have faith."

I let no one go with me but Peter, James, and James's

brother John. We came to the house of the leader of the synagogue, and there I saw the flute-players and found everything in confusion, and people weeping and wailing. And I went into the house and said to them,

"What is the meaning of all this confusion and crying? The child is not dead, she is asleep." And they laughed at me. But I drove them all out, and took the child's father and mother and the men who were with me and went into the room where the child was lying. I grasped her hand and said to her,

"Taleitha, koum!"—that is to say, "Little girl, I tell you, get up!"

And the little girl immediately got up and walked about, for she was twelve years old. The moment they saw it they were utterly amazed. And I strictly forbade them to let anyone know of it, and told them to give her something to eat.

Healings by the Way

As I was passing along from there, two blind men followed me, calling out,

"Take pity on us, you Son of David!"

When I had gone indoors, the blind men came up to me, and I said to them,

"Do you believe that I can do this?"

They said to me,

"Yes, sir."

Then I touched their eyes and said,

"You shall have what your faith expects."

And their sight was restored. I warned them sternly not to let anyone hear of it. But they went out and spread the news about me all over that part of the country.

But just as they were going out, some people brought to me a dumb man who was possessed by a demon, and as soon as the demon was driven out, the dumb man was able to speak. And the crowds were amazed, and said,

"Nothing like this was ever seen in Israel!"

But the Pharisees said,

"It is by the aid of the prince of the demons that he drives them out."

WIDER EVANGELIZATION OF GALILEE

A Visit to My Home

And I came to Nazareth, where I had been brought up, and on the Sabbath I went to the synagogue, as I was accustomed to do, and stood up to read the Scriptures. And the roll of the prophet Isaiah was handed to me, and I unrolled it and found the place where it says,

> "The spirit of the Lord is upon me,
>> For he has consecrated me to preach the good news to the poor,
>> He has sent me to announce to the prisoners their release and to the blind the recovery of their sight,
>> To set the down-trodden at liberty,
>> To proclaim the year of the Lord's favor!"

And I rolled up the roll and gave it back to the attendant and sat down. The eyes of everyone in the synagogue were fixed upon me. And I began by saying to them,

"This passage of Scripture has been fulfilled here in your hearing today!"

And they all spoke well of me. They were astonished at the winning words that fell from my lips, and they said,

"Where did he get all this? How does he come to have such wisdom? How are such marvelous things done through him? Is he not the carpenter, Mary's son, and the brother of James, Joses, Judas, and Simon? And do not his sisters live here among us?"

And they took offense at me. I said to them,

"No doubt you will quote this proverb to me: 'Doctor, cure yourself! Do the things here in your own country that we hear you did at Capernaum.' I tell you," said I, "no prophet is welcome in his own country. But I tell you, there were plenty of widows in Israel in Elijah's time, when the sky was closed for three years and a half, and there was a great famine all over the land, and Elijah was not sent to one of them, but to a widow at Zarephath in Sidon. And there were plenty of lepers in Israel in the time of the prophet Elisha, and none of them was cured, but Naaman the Syrian."

And when the people in the synagogue heard this, they were all very angry, and they got up and drove me out of the town and took me to the brow of the hill on which their town was built, intending to throw me down from it. But I made my way through the midst of them and went on.

I could not do any wonder there in Nazareth, except that I put my hands on a few sick people and cured them.

Preaching in the Villages

I went round among all the towns and villages, teaching in their synagogues, and proclaiming the good news of the kingdom, and curing any disease or illness.

But the sight of the crowds of people filled me with pity for them, because they were bewildered and dejected, like sheep that have no shepherd. Then I said to my disciples,

"The harvest is abundant, but the reapers are few. So pray to the owner of the harvest to send reapers to gather it."

The Twelve Sent Forth

I called the Twelve to me and sent them off two by two, giving them power over the foul spirits so that they could drive them out, and so that they could heal any disease or illness. I gave them these directions:

"Do not go among the heathen, or to any Samaritan town, but proceed instead to the lost sheep of Israel's house. And as you go about, preach and say, 'The Kingdom of Heaven is at hand!' Cure the sick, raise the dead, heal lepers, drive out demons. Give without payment, just as you received without payment. Do not accept gold or silver or copper money to put in your pockets, and do not take a bag for your journey, nor two shirts, nor shoes nor a staff, for the workman deserves his food! Whatever town or village you come to, inquire for some suitable person, and stay with him till you leave the place. And as you go into his house, wish it well. If the house deserves it, the peace you wish it will come over it, but if it does not deserve it, your blessing will come back upon yourselves. And where no one will welcome you, or listen to you, leave that house or town and shake off its very dust from your feet. I tell you, the land of Sodom and Gomorrah will fare better on the Day of Judgment than that town.

"Here I am sending you out like sheep among wolves. So you must be wise like serpents, and guileless like doves. But be on your guard against men, for they will give you up to their courts, and have you flogged in their synagogues, and you will be brought before governors and kings on my account, to bear your testimony before them and the heathen. But when they give you up, you must have no anxiety about how to speak or what to say, for you will be told at the very moment what you ought to say, for it is not you who will speak, it is the Spirit of your Father that will speak through you. One brother will give up another to death, and a father his child, and children will turn against their parents, and have them put to death. You

[71]

will be hated by everybody on my account, but the man who holds out to the very end will be saved. But when they persecute you in one town, make your escape to another, for I tell you, you will not have gone through all the towns of Israel before the Son of Man arrives.

"A pupil is not better than his teacher, nor a slave better than his master. A pupil should be satisfied to come to be like his teacher, or a slave to come to be like his master. If men have called the head of the house Beelzebub, how much worse names will they give to the members of his household! So do not be afraid of them. For there is nothing covered up that is not going to be uncovered, nor secret that is not going to be known. What I tell you in the dark you must say in the light, and what you hear whispered in your ear, you must proclaim from the housetops. Have no fear of those who kill the body, but cannot kill the soul. You had better be afraid of one who can destroy both soul and body in the pit. Do not sparrows sell two for a cent? And yet not one of them can fall to the ground against your Father's will! But the very hairs on your heads are all counted. You must not be afraid; you are worth more than a great many sparrows! Therefore everyone who will acknowledge me before my Father in heaven, but anyone who disowns me before men, I will disown before my Father in heaven.

"I have come to bring fire down to the earth, and how I wish it were kindled already! I have a baptism to undergo, and how distressed I am till it is over!

"Do not think that I have come to bring peace to the earth. I have not come to bring peace but a sword. For I have come to turn a man against his father and a daughter against her mother and a daughter-in-law against her mother-in-law, and a man's enemies will be in his own household. No one who loves father or mother more than he loves me is worthy of me, and no one who loves son or daughter more than he loves me is worthy of me, and no one who will not take up his cross and follow me is worthy of me. Whoever gains his life will lose it, and whoever loses his life for my sake will gain it.

"Whoever welcomes you welcomes me, and whoever welcomes me welcomes him who has sent me. Whoever welcomes a prophet because he is a prophet will have the same reward

as a prophet, and whoever welcomes an upright man because
he is upright will have the same reward as an upright man.
And no one who will give the humblest of my disciples even a
cup of cold water because he is my disciple, I tell you, can ever
fail of his reward."

And the twelve set forth and went from village to village,
telling the good news and curing people everywhere, and drove
out many demons and cured many sick people by anointing
them with oil.

At that time, Herod the governor heard the reports about
me, and he said to his attendants,

"This man must be John the Baptist. He has risen from the
dead, and that is why wonderful powers are working through
him." But others said I was Elijah, and still others that I was
a prophet of the old prophetic kind. But Herod said,

"John, I have beheaded, but who can this be about whom I
hear such reports?"

And he endeavored to see me.

THE CRISIS IN CAPERNAUM

The Five Thousand Fed

The apostles rejoined me and reported to me all they had done
and taught. Now the Jewish festival of the Passover was coming. And I said to them,

"Come away by yourselves to some quiet place, and rest a
little while."

For people were coming and going in large numbers, and
we had no time even for meals. So we set off by ourselves in
their boat for a secluded place. And many people saw us start
and knew of it, and hurried around by land from all the neighboring towns, and got ahead of us. So when we got out of the
boat we found a great crowd gathered, and I welcomed them

[73]

and spoke to them about the Kingdom of God, and I cured those who needed to be cured. My heart was touched at the sight of them, because they were like sheep that have no shepherd, and I proceeded to teach them a great deal. When the day began to decline, the Twelve came up and said to me,

"Send the crowd away to the villages and farms around to find food and shelter, for we are in a lonely place here."

But I said to them,

"They do not need to go away. Give them food yourselves."

Philip answered,

"Forty dollars' worth of bread would not be enough for each of them to have even a little."

But I said to them,

"How many loaves have you? Go and see."

Andrew, Simon Peter's brother, another of my disciples, said to me,

"There is a boy here who has five barley loaves and a couple of fish, but what is that among so many people?"

I said,

"Bring them here to me."

And I directed them all to sit down in parties on the fresh grass. So they threw themselves down in groups, in hundreds and in fifties. Then I took the five loaves and the two fish and looked up to heaven and blessed the loaves and broke them in pieces and gave them to the disciples to pass to the people; and I divided the two fish among them all. And they all ate and had enough. And the pieces they gathered up filled twelve baskets, besides the pieces of the fish. There were five thousand men who ate the loaves.

When the people saw the signs that I showed, they said,

"This is really the Prophet who was to come into the world!"

I saw that they meant to come and carry me off to make me their king. So I made my disciples get into the boat and cross before me to the other side while I dismissed the crowds. After I had dismissed them I went up the hill by myself to pray. And when evening came on I was there alone.

My disciples started across the sea for Capernaum. By this time it was dark, and I had not yet joined them; a strong wind was blowing and the sea was growing rough. Toward morning

I went out to them, walking on the sea. When they had rowed three or four miles, they saw me walking on the sea and approaching the boat, and they were terrified, and said,

"It is a ghost!"

And they screamed with fear. But I immediately spoke to them and said,

"Take courage! It is I. Do not be afraid."

Peter answered,

"If it is you, Master, order me to come to you on the water."

And I said,

"Come!"

And Peter got out of the boat and walked on the water and came to me. But when he felt the wind he was frightened, and beginning to sink, he cried out,

"Master, save me!"

I immediately stretched out my hand and caught hold of him, and said to him,

"Why did you waver? You have so little faith!"

When we got into the boat, the wind went down. My disciples were greatly astonished, for they had not understood about the loaves, but their minds were blinded.

We crossed over to the other side and came to Gennesaret and moored the boat. As soon as we came ashore, and the people recognized me, they hurried all over the countryside and began to bring the sick to me on their mats, wherever they heard I was.

The Disappointment of the People

Next day the people who had stayed on the other side of the sea saw that there had been only one boat there, and that I had not embarked in it with my disciples, but that the disciples had gone away by themselves. But some boats from Tiberias landed near the place where we had eaten the bread after I had given thanks for it. So when the people saw that neither I nor my disciples were any longer there, they got into the boats and went to Capernaum in search of me. And when they had crossed the sea and found me, they said to me,

"When did you get here, Master?"

I answered,

"I tell you, it is not because of the signs you have seen that you have come in search of me, but because you ate that bread and had all you wanted of it. You must not work for the food that perishes, but for that which lasts for eternal life, which the Son of Man will give you, for God the Father has authorized him to do so."

Then they said to me,

"What must we do to carry out God's work?"

I answered them,

"The work God has for you is to believe in the messenger that he has sent to you."

Then they said to me,

"Then what sign will you show us so we will come to believe you? What work will you do? Our forefathers in the desert had manna to eat; as the Scripture says, 'He gave them bread out of heaven to eat!' "

I said to them,

"I tell you, Moses did not give you the bread out of heaven, but my Father gives you the bread out of heaven; for God's bread comes down out of heaven and gives life to the world."

Then they said to me,

"Give us that bread always, sir!"

I said to them,

"I am the bread that gives life. No one who comes to me will ever be hungry, and no one who believes in me will ever be thirsty. But as I have told you, although you have seen me, you do not believe. All that my Father gives to me will come to me, and I will never refuse anyone who comes to me, for I have come down from heaven not to do what I please but what pleases him who has sent me. And the purpose of him who has sent me is this, that I should lose nothing of all that he has given me, but should raise them to life on the Last Day. For it is the purpose of my Father that everyone who sees the Son and believes in him shall have eternal life, and that I shall raise him to life on the Last Day."

The Jews complained of me for saying, "I am the bread that has come out of heaven," and they said,

"Is he not Joseph's son, Jesus, whose father and mother we know? How can he now say, 'I have come down out of heaven'?"

I answered,

"Do not complain to one another. No one can come to me unless the Father who sent me draws him to me; then I myself will raise him to life on the Last Day. In the prophets it is written, 'And all men will be taught by God!' Everyone who listens to the Father and learns from him will come to me. Not that anyone has ever seen the Father, except him who is from God; he has seen the Father. I tell you, whoever believes already possesses eternal life. I am the bread that gives life. Your forefathers in the desert ate the manna and yet they died. But here is bread that comes down out of heaven, and no one who eats it will ever die. I am this living bread that has come down out of heaven. Whoever eats this bread will live forever, and the bread that I will give for the world's life is my own flesh!"

This led the Jews to dispute with one another. They said,

"How can he give us his flesh to eat?"

Then I said to them,

"I tell you, if you do not eat the flesh of the Son of Man and drink his blood, you have no self-existent life. Whoever lives on my flesh and drinks my blood possesses eternal life, and I will raise him to life on the Last Day. For my flesh is real food and my blood is real drink. Whoever lives on my flesh and drinks my blood remains united to me and I remain united to him. Just as the living Father has sent me, and I live because of the Father, so he who lives on me will live because of me. This is the bread that has come down out of heaven—not like that which your forefathers ate and yet died. Whoever lives on this bread will live forever."

I said all this while I was teaching in the synagogue at Capernaum.

Many of my disciples on hearing it said,

"This is a harsh teaching! Who can listen to it?"

But I knew that my disciples were complaining about this, and I said to them,

"Does this stagger you? Then what if you see the Son of Man go up where he was before? The Spirit is what gives life; flesh is of no use at all. The things that I have said to you are spirit and they are life. Yet there are some of you who will not believe." For I knew from the first who would not believe, and who was going to betray me. And I added.

"This is why I said to you, 'No one can come to me unless he is enabled to do so by the Father.' "

In consequence of this many of my disciples drew back and would not go about with me any longer. So I said to the Twelve,

"Do you mean to go away too?"

Simon Peter answered,

"To whom can we go, sir? You have the message of eternal life, and we believe and are satisfied that you are the Holy One of God."

I answered them,

"Did I not myself select all twelve of you? And even of you, one is an informer." I meant Judas the son of Simon Iscariot, for he, though he was one of the Twelve, was going to betray me.

I Reject the Tradition of the Elders

The Pharisees gathered about me with some scribes who had come from Jerusalem. They had noticed that some of my disciples ate their food without first giving their hands a ceremonial washing to purify them. For the Pharisees and all the Jews observe the rules handed down from their ancestors, and will not eat until they have washed their hands in a particular way, and they will not eat anything from the market without first purifying it by sprinkling it, and they have a number of other observances which have come to them, in the way of washing cups, pitchers, and basins. And the Pharisees and the scribes asked me,

"Why do your disciples not observe the rules handed down by our ancestors, but eat food without purifying their hands?"

But I said to them,

"It was about you hypocrites that Isaiah prophesied so finely, in the words,

" 'This people honor me with their lips,
Yet their hearts are far away from me.
But their worship of me is all in vain,
For the lessons they teach are but human precepts.'

"You give up what God has commanded and hold fast to what men have handed down.

"How skilful you are," I said to them, "in nullifying what God has commanded in order to observe what has been handed down to you. For Moses said, 'Honor your father and your mother,' and again, 'Whoever abuses his father or mother must be put to death.' But you say, 'If a man says to his father or mother, "Anything of mine that might have been of use to you is Korban," ' that is, consecrated to God, you let that man off from doing anything more for his father or mother. So you nullify what God has said by what you have handed down. You have many such practices."

I called the people to me again and said to them,

"Listen to me, all of you, and understand this. Nothing that goes into a man from outside can pollute him. It is what comes out of a man that pollutes him."

Then my disciples came up to me and said to me,

"Do you know that the Pharisees were shocked to hear you say that?"

But I answered,

"Any plant that my heavenly Father did not plant must be uprooted! Leave them alone. They are blind guides! But if one blind man leads another, they will both fall into the ditch!"

When I had left the crowd and gone home, my disciples asked me what I meant by this figure. And I said to them,

"Have not even you any understanding then? Do you not see that nothing that goes into a man from outside can pollute him, since it does not go into his heart but into his stomach and then is disposed of?" So I declared all food clean. I went on to say,

"It is what comes out of a man that pollutes him. For it is from inside, from men's hearts, that designs of evil come; immorality, stealing, murder, adultery, greed, malice, deceit, indecency, envy, abusiveness, arrogance, folly—all these evils come from inside, and they pollute a man. But not eating with unwashed hands!"

The Plot of the Pharisees

On another Sabbath I happened to go to the synagogue and teach. There was a man there whose right hand was withered. And the scribes and the Pharisees were on the watch to see whether I would cure people on the Sabbath, in order to find a charge to bring against me. But I knew what they were thinking, and I said to the man with the withered hand,

"Get up and stand in front."

And he got up and stood there. I said to them,

"I want to ask you, is it allowable on the Sabbath to do people good or to do them harm? to save life or to destroy it? Who among you if he has even a single sheep and it falls into a hole on the Sabbath, will not take hold of it and lift it out? And how much more a man is worth than a sheep! Therefore, it is right to do people good on the Sabbath."

But they made no answer. And I looked around at them with anger, hurt by their obstinacy, and I said to the man,

"Hold out your hand!" And he held it out, and it was restored and became as well as the other.

But they were perfectly furious, and discussed with one another what they could do to me. Then the Pharisees left the synagogue and immediately consulted with the Herodians about me, with a view to putting me to death.

MY WITHDRAWAL WITH THE TWELVE

The Ministry Beyond Galilee

So I left that place and went to the neighborhood of Tyre and Sidon. There I went into a certain house, and wanted no one to know of it. But I could not keep it secret. A woman whose little daughter was possessed by a foul spirit immediately heard about me and came and threw herself at my feet. Now the woman was a Greek, of Syrophoenician birth. And she screamed:

"Son of David, take pity on me, sir! My daughter is dreadfully possessed by a demon!"

But I would not answer her a word. And my disciples came up and urged me, saying,

"Send her away, for she keeps screaming after us."

But I answered,

"I am sent only to the lost sheep of Israel's house."

And she came and fell down before me, and said,

"Help me, sir!"

I said to her,

"Let the children first eat all they want, for it is not right to take the children's bread and throw it to the dogs."

But she answered,

"True, sir! and still the dogs under the table eat what the children leave!"

Then I answered,

"You have great faith! You shall have what you want. Go home; the demon has left your daughter."

And she went home and found the child lying on the bed, and the demon gone.

I left the neighborhood of Tyre again and went by way of
Sidon to the Sea of Galilee, crossing the district of the Ten
Towns, and went up on the hillside and sat down there. Then
great crowds came to me bringing with them those who were
lame, crippled, blind, or dumb, and many others. And they
laid them down at my feet, and I cured them, so that the
people were astonished to see the dumb speak, the lame walk
and the blind see. And they praised the God of Israel.

They brought to me a man who was deaf and hardly able
to speak, and they begged me to lay my hand on him. I took
him off by himself away from the crowd, and put my fingers
in the man's ears, and touched his tongue with saliva. And I
looked up to heaven and sighed, and said to him,

"Ephphatha!" —which means "Open."

And his ears were opened and his tongue was released and
he talked plainly. And I forbade them to tell anyone about it,
but the more I forbade them the more they spread the news
far and wide. And people were utterly amazed, and said,

"How well he has done everything! He even makes the deaf
hear and the dumb speak!"

THE FOUR THOUSAND FED

In those days when a great crowd had gathered again and
they had nothing to eat, I called my disciples to me and said
to them,

"I pity these people, for they have been staying with me
three days now, and they have nothing left to eat. And if I

send them home hungry they will give out on the way, for some of them come from a distance."

My disciples replied,

"Where can anyone get bread enough, here in this solitude, to satisfy these people's hunger?"

"How many loaves have you?" I asked.

"Seven," they said,

Then I ordered the people to take their places on the ground. And I took the seven loaves and gave thanks and broke them in pieces and gave them to my disciples to pass, and they passed them to the people. They had a few small fish, and I blessed them and told the disciples to pass them also to the people. And they ate and satisfied their hunger. And the pieces that they left, that were picked up, filled seven baskets. There were four thousand men who were fed, besides women and children. And I dismissed the people and got into the boat and went to the district of Magadan.

The Pharisees and Sadducees Demand a Sign

The Pharisees came out and began a discussion with me, testing me by asking me to show them a sign from heaven. And I sighed deeply and said,

"Why do the men of this day ask for a sign? I tell you, no sign will be given them."

And I left them and got into the boat again and crossed to the other side.

Now they had forgotten to bring any bread, and they had only one loaf with them in the boat. And I warned them, saying,

"Look out! Be on your guard against the yeast of the Pharisees and the yeast of Herod!"

They were discussing with one another their being without bread. And I noticed it and said to them,

"Why do you discuss your being without bread? Do you not yet see nor understand? Are your minds so dull? When you

[83]

have eyes can you not see, and when you have ears can you not hear? Do you not remember how many baskets of pieces you picked up when I broke the five loaves in pieces for those five thousand men?"

They said to me,

"Twelve."

"Nor the seven loaves for the four thousand, and how many baskets full you gathered up? Why do you not see that I was not talking to you about bread? But be on your guard against the yeast of the Pharisees and Sadducees!"

Then they understood that I was warning them not against yeast but against the teaching of the Pharisees and Sadducees.

The Blind Man Healed

We came to Bethsaida. And people brought a blind man to me and begged me to touch him. I took him by the hand and led him outside of the village, and spitting in his eyes I laid my hands on him and asked him,

"Do you see anything?"

He looked up and said,

"I can see people, for they look to me like trees, only they are moving about."

Then I laid my hands on his eyes again, and he looked steadily and was cured, and saw everything plainly. And I sent him home and said to him,

"Do not even go into the village."

THE MESSIAH

Peter's Confession

Then my disciples and I went away to the villages around
Caesarea Philippi. On the way I questioned my disciples and
said to them,

"Who do the people say that I am?"

They answered,

"John the Baptist, though others say Elijah, and still others
Jeremiah or that one of the old prophets has come back to
life."

I said to them,

"But who do you say that I am?"

Simon Peter answered,

"You are the Christ, the Son of the living God!"

I answered,

"Blessed are you, Simon, son of Jonah, for human nature
has not disclosed this to you, but my Father in heaven! But I
tell you, your name is Peter, a rock, and on this rock I will
build my church, and the powers of death shall not subdue it.
I will give you the keys of the Kingdom of Heaven, and whatever you forbid on earth will be held in heaven to be forbidden, and whatever you permit on earth will be held in
heaven to be permitted."

The Passion and Resurrection Foretold

It was then that I for the first time explained to my disciples that I had to go to Jerusalem and endure great suffering there at the hands of the elders, high priests, and scribes, and be killed, and be raised to life on the third day. And Peter took me aside, and began to reprove me for it. But turning and seeing my disciples I reproved Peter, and said,

"Get out of my sight, you Satan! You hinder me, for you do not side with God, but with men!"

And I called the people and my disciples to me and said to them,

"If anyone wants to go with me, he must disregard himself, and take his cross and follow me. For whoever wants to preserve his own life will lose it, and whoever loses his life for me and for the good news will preserve it. For what good does it do a man to gain the whole world and yet part with his life? For what can a man give to buy back his life? For if anyone is ashamed of me and my teaching in this unfaithful and sinful age, then the Son of Man will be ashamed of him, when he comes back in his Father's glory, with the holy angels. I tell you, some of you who stand here will certainly live to see the reign of God come in its might."

The Transfiguration

It was about eight days after I said this that I took Peter, John, and James, and went up on the mountain to pray. And as I was praying, my appearance underwent a change in their presence and my face shone like the sun, and my clothes became as white as light. And Moses and Elijah appeared to them, talking with me about my departure which I was to go through with at Jerusalem. Peter and his companions had been overcome by sleep, but waking up they saw my glorious appearance and the two men standing by me. Just as they were parting from me, Peter said to me:

"Master, how good it is that we are here! Let us put up three huts, one for you and one for Moses and one for Elijah!" For he did not know what he was saying.

As he spoke a bright cloud overshadowed us and a voice from the cloud said,

"This is my Son, my Beloved. He is my Chosen. Listen to him!"

When the disciples heard it, they were dreadfully frightened and fell upon their faces. And I came and touched them, and said,

"Get up and do not be afraid."

And suddenly, on looking around, they saw that there was now no one with us but I alone. As we were going down the mountain, I cautioned them to let no one know what they had seen, until the Son of Man should rise from the dead. And they did not forget what I said, but discussed with one another what I meant by the rising from the dead. And they asked me,

"Why do the scribes say that Elijah has to come first?"

I said to them,

"Elijah does come first, and reforms everything, and does not the Scripture say of the Son of Man that he will suffer much and be refused? Why, I tell you, not only has Elijah come, but people have treated him just as they pleased, as the Scripture says about him."

Then the disciples understood that I was speaking to them of John the Baptist.

The Epileptic Boy

When we came to the disciples, we saw a great crowd around them, and some scribes arguing with them. And all the people were amazed when they saw me, and they ran up and greeted me. And I asked them,

"What are you discussing with them?"

And a man in the crowd shouted,

"Master, I beg you to look at my son, for he is my only child. Take pity on my son, for he has epilepsy and is very wretched; he often falls into the fire or into the water. I brought him to your disciples and they have not been able to cure him."

I answered,

"O you unbelieving, obstinate people! How long must I be with you? How long must I put up with you? Bring him here to me!"

And they brought the boy to me. As soon as the spirit saw me, it convulsed the boy, and he fell down on the ground and rolled about, foaming at the mouth. I asked the boy's father,

"How long has he been like this?"

And he said,

"From his childhood, and many a time it has thrown him into the fire or into the water, to put an end to him. But if there is anything you can do, take pity on us and help us!"

I said to him,

" 'If there is anything I can do!' Everything is possible for one who has faith!"

The boy's father immediately cried out,

"I have faith! Help my want of faith!"

Then I, seeing that a crowd was rapidly gathering, reproved the foul spirit and said to it,

"You deaf and dumb spirit, get out of him, I charge you, and never enter him again!"

And it gave a cry and convulsed him terribly, and went out of him. And the boy was like a corpse, so that most of them said that he was dead. But I grasped his hand and made him rise, and he stood up. When he had gone home, and my disciples were alone with me, they asked me,

"Why could not we drive it out?"

I said to them,

"This kind of thing can be driven out only by prayer. For I tell you, if you have faith the size of a grain of mustard, you can say to this mountain, 'Move from here over to there!' and it will move and nothing will be impossible for you."

THE TRAINING OF THE TWELVE

The Passion and Resurrection Again Foretold

We left that place and made our way through Galilee, and I did not wish anyone to know it; for I was teaching my disciples, saying to them,

"The Son of Man is to be handed over to men, and they will kill him, and three days after he is killed he will rise again."

But they did not understand what I meant, and they were afraid to ask me about it.

The Greatest Disciple

We returned to Capernaum. When we reached home, I asked them,

"What was it that you were discussing on the way?"

But they made no answer, for on the way they had been discussing with one another which of them was the greatest. And I sat down and called the Twelve in, and said to them,

"If anyone wishes to be first, he must be the last of all and the servant of all."

And I took a child and made him stand among us, and I put my arms around him, and said to them,

"I tell you, unless you change and become like children, you will never get into the Kingdom of Heaven at all. Anyone, therefore, who is as unassuming as this child is the greatest in the Kingdom of Heaven, and anyone who welcomes one child like this on my account welcomes me, and whoever welcomes me, welcomes not me but him who has sent me."

John said to me,

"Master, we saw a man driving out demons with your name, and we told him not to do so, for he was not one of our followers."

But I said,

"Do not tell him not to do so, for there is no one who will use my name to do a mighty act, and be able soon after to abuse me. For the man who is not against us is for us. For whoever gives you a cup of water to drink, on the ground that you belong to Christ, I tell you, will certainly not fail to be repaid. But whoever hinders one of these children who believe in me might better have a great millstone hung around his neck and be sunk in the open sea. Alas for the world for such hindrances! They have to come, but alas for the man who causes them!

"But if your own hand or your own foot makes you fall, cut it off and throw it away. You might better enter upon life maimed or crippled than keep both hands and feet but be thrown into the everlasting fire. And if your own eye makes you fall, dig it out and throw it away. You might better enter upon life with only one eye than be thrown with both eyes into the fiery pit, where the worm that feeds upon them never dies and the fire is never put out. Everyone must be seasoned with fire. Salt is a good thing, but if salt loses its strength, what will you use to season it? You must have salt within you, and live in peace with one another.

"Beware of feeling scornful of one single little child, for I tell you that in heaven their angels have continual access to my Father in heaven. What do you think? If a man has a hundred sheep and one of them strays away, will he not leave the ninety-nine on the hills, and go in search of the one that is astray? And if he happens to find it, I tell you he rejoices more over it than he does over the ninety-nine that did not stray. In just that way, it is the will of my Father in heaven that not a single one of these children be lost.

Forgiveness

"If your brother wrongs you," I told my disciples, "go to him and show him his fault while you are alone with him. If he listens to you, you have won back your brother. But if he will not listen, take one or two others with you, so that everything may be supported by the testimony of two or three witnesses. If he refuses to listen to them, tell the congregation. And if he refuses to listen to it, treat him as a heathen or a tax-collector.

"I tell you, whatever you forbid on earth will be held in heaven to be forbidden, and whatever you permit on earth will be held in heaven to be permitted. Again, I tell you, if even two of you here on earth agree about what they shall pray for, it will be given them by my Father in heaven. For wherever two or three are gathered as my followers, I am there among them."

Then Peter came and asked,

"Master, how many times am I to forgive my brother when he wrongs me? Seven times over?"

I said to him,

"Not seven times over, I tell you, but seventy-seven times over! For this reason the Kingdom of Heaven may be compared to a king, who resolved to settle accounts with his slaves. And when he set about doing so, a man was brought in who owed him ten million dollars. And as he could not pay, his master ordered him to be sold, with his wife and children and all he had, in payment of the debt. So the slave threw himself down before him and implored him, 'Give me time, and I will pay you all of it.' And his master's heart was touched, and he let the slave go and cancelled the debt. But when the slave went out he met a fellow-slave of his who owed him twenty dollars, and he caught him by the throat and began to choke him, saying, 'Pay me what you owe!' So his fellow-slave threw himself down before him, and begged him, 'Give me time, and I will pay you.' But he refused and went and had him put in prison until he should pay the debt. When his fellow-slaves saw what had happened, they were greatly distressed, and they went to their master and reported the whole matter to him. Then his master called him in and said to him, 'You wicked slave! I cancelled all that debt of yours when you entreated me. Ought you not to have taken pity on your fellow-slave, as I did on you?' So his master in his anger handed him over to the jailers, until he should pay all he owed him. That is what my heavenly Father will do to you, if you do not each forgive your brothers from your hearts!"

The Sheckel for the Temple

The collectors of the temple-tax came and said to Peter, "Does not your Master pay the temple-tax?"
He said,
"Yes."
But when we went home, I spoke of it first and said,
"What do you think, Simon? From whom do earthly kings collect duties and taxes? From their own people, or from aliens?"
He said,
"From aliens."
I said to him,
"Then their own people are exempt. But rather than give offense to them, go down to the sea and throw in a hook. Take the first fish that comes up, open its mouth and you will find in it a dollar. Take that and pay the tax for us both."

MY FACE TOWARD JERUSALEM

The Final Departure from Galilee

The Jewish camping festival was coming. So my brothers said to me,

"You ought to leave here and go to Judea, to let your disciples also see the things you are doing. For no one acts in secret when he desires to be publicly known. If you are going to do these things, let the world see you." For even my brothers did not believe in me. Then I said to them,

"It is not yet time for me to act, but any time is suitable for you. It is impossible for the world to hate you, but it does hate me for testifying that its ways are wrong. As for you, go up to the festival; I am not going up to this festival as yet, for it is not quite time for me to go."

That was what I told them, and I stayed on in Galilee.

As the time approached when I was to be taken up to heaven, I set my face toward Jerusalem, and sent messengers before me. They started out and went into a Samaritan village, to make preparations for me. And the people there would not receive me, because I was going to Jerusalem. When the disciples, James and John, saw this, they said,

"Master, will you have us order fire to come down from heaven and consume them?"

But I turned and reproved them. And we went on to another village.

The Grateful Samaritan Leper

On the way to Jerusalem, we passed through Samaria and Galilee. And as we were going into one village we met ten lepers, and they stood at some distance from us, and raising their voices, said

"Jesus, Master, take pity on us!"

And when I saw them, I said to them,

"Go and show yourselves to the priests."

And as they went they were cured. But one of them, when he saw that he was cured, came back, loudly praising God, and fell on his face at my feet, and thanked me. He was a Samaritan. And I said,

"Were not all ten cured? Where are the other nine? Was no one found to return and give thanks to God except this foreigner?"

And I said to him,

"Stand up and go! Your faith has cured you."

New Disciples

As we were going along the road, a man said to me,

"I will follow you wherever you go."

"I said to him,

"Foxes have holes, and wild birds have nests, but the Son of Man has nowhere to lay his head!"

I said to another,

"Follow me."

But he said,

"Let me first go and bury my father."

I said to him,

"Leave the dead to bury their own dead; you must go and spread the news of the Kingdom of God!"

Yet another man said to me,

"Master, I am going to follow you, but let me first say goodbye to my people at home."

I said to him,

"No one who puts his hand to the plough, and then looks back, is fitted for the Kingdom of God."

IN JERUSALEM—THE ATTEMPT TO STONE ME

At the Feast of Tabernacles

But after my brothers had gone up to the festival, then I went up also, not publicly, but as though I did not wish to be observed. Now the Jews were looking for me at the festival and asking where I was, and there was a great deal of muttering about me among the crowds, some saying that I was a good man, and others that I was not, but was imposing on the people. But no one spoke of me in public, for fear of the Jews.

But when the festival was half over, I went up to the Temple and began to teach. This astonished the Jews.

"How is it that this man can read" they said, "when he has never gone to school?"

So I answered,

"My teaching is not my own; it comes from him who has sent me. Anyone who resolves to do his will will know whether my teaching comes from God, or originates with me. Whoever speaks simply for himself is looking for honor for himself, but whoever looks for honor for the person who has sent him shows his sincerity; there is no dishonesty about him. Was it not Moses who gave you the Law? Yet not one of you obeys the Law. Why are you trying to kill me?"

The crowd answered,

"You must be possessed! Who is trying to kill you?"

I answered,

"I have done just one deed on the Sabbath and you are all astonished at it. Yet Moses gave you the rite of circumcision—not that it began with Moses but with your forefathers—and you practice it even on the Sabbath. But if a person undergoes circumcision on a Sabbath, to avoid breaking the Law of Moses, are you angry at me for making a man perfectly well on a Sabbath? You must not judge so externally; you must judge justly!"

Some of the people of Jerusalem said,

"Is not this the man they want to kill? And here he is speaking publicly, and they say nothing to him! Can the authorities really have found that he is the Christ? But then, we know where this man comes from, but when the Christ comes, no one will know where he is from."

As I was teaching in the Temple, I cried out,

"You do know me and you know where I come from, and I have not come of my own accord but someone who is very real, whom you do not know, has sent me. I do know him, because I come from him, and he has sent me here."

Then they tried to arrest me, and yet no one laid hands on me, because I was not yet ready. But many of the people believed in me, and said,

"Will the Christ show more signs when he comes than this man has shown?"

The Pharisees heard the people saying these things about me in whispers, and the high priests and the Pharisees sent attendants to arrest me. I said,

"I am to be with you a little while longer, and then I am going to him who has sent me. You will look for me and you will not find me, and you will not be able to go where I shall be."

Then the Jews said to one another,

"Where is he going, that we shall not find him? Is he going to our people scattered among the Greeks, and will he teach the Greeks? What does he mean by saying 'You will look for me and you will not find me, and you will not be able to go where I shall be'?"

Now on the last day, the great day of the festival, I stood up and cried out,

"If anyone is thirsty, let him come to me and drink. If anyone believes in me, streams of living water, as the Scripture says, shall flow forth from his heart."

I meant by this the Spirit which those who believed in me were to receive—for the Spirit had not yet come, because I had not yet been glorified. So some of the people, when they heard these words, said,

"This is certainly the Prophet!"

Others said,

"This is the Christ!"

But they replied,

"What! Is the Christ to come from Galilee? Do not the Scriptures say that the Christ is to spring from the descendants of David and to come from the village of Bethlehem where David lived?"

So the people were divided about me, and some of them wanted to arrest me, yet no one laid hands on me.

The attendants went back to the high priests and Pharisees, and they said to the attendants,

"Why have you not brought him?"

The attendants answered,

"No man ever talked as he does!"

The Pharisees answered,

"Have you been imposed upon too? Have any of the authorities or of the Pharisees believed in him? But these common people who do not know the Law are doomed!"

One of them, Nicodemus, who had previously come to me, said to them,

"Does our Law condemn the accused without first hearing what he has to say, and finding out what he has done?"

They answered,

"Are you from Galilee too? Study and you will find that no prophet is to appear from Galilee."

Then I spoke to them again and said,

"I am the light of the world. Whoever follows me will not have to walk in darkness but will have the light of life."

The Pharisees said to me,

"You are testifying to yourself. Your testimony is not true."

I answered,

"Even if I am testifying to myself, my testimony is true, for I know where I have come from and where I am going; but you do not know where I come from or where I am going. You judge by material standards, but I am judging nobody. But even if I do judge, my decision is just, because I am not by myself, but the Father who sent me is with me. Why, in your own Law it is stated that the testimony of two persons is valid. Here I am testifying to myself, and the Father who has sent me testifies to me."

Then they said to me,

"Where is your Father?"

I answered,

"You do not know either me or my Father. If you knew me, you would know my Father too."

I said these things in the treasury, as I was teaching in the Temple, and no one arrested me, because I was not yet ready.

Then I said to them again,

"I am going away, and you will look for me, but you will die in the midst of your sin. You cannot come where I am going."

So the Jews said,

"Is he going to kill himself, and is that why he says, 'You cannot come where I am going'?"

I said to them,

"You are from below; I am from above. You belong to this world; I do not belong to this world. That is why I said to you that you would die in the midst of your sins, for unless you believe that I am what I say, you will die in the midst of your sins."

They said to me,

"Who are you?"

I said to them,

"Why do I even talk to you at all? I have a great deal to say about you and to condemn in you, yet he who sent me is truthful, and the things that I say to the world are things that I have learned from him."

They did not understand that I was speaking to them of the Father. So I said,

"When you lift the Son of Man up in the air, then you will know that I am what I say, and that I do nothing of my own accord, but speak as the Father has instructed me. And he who has sent me is with me; he has not left me alone, for I always do what pleases him."

As I said this, many believed in me.

The Freedom of the Soul

So I said to the Jews who had believed in me,

"If you abide by what I teach, you are really disciples of mine, and you will know the truth and the truth will set you free."

They answered,

"We are descended from Abraham, and have never been anyone's slaves. How can you say to us, 'You will be set free'?"

I answered,

"I tell you, everyone who commits sin is a slave to sin. Now a slave does not belong to a household permanently; but a son does. So if the Son sets you free you will be really free. I know that you are descended from Abraham, yet you want to kill me, because there is no room in your hearts for my teaching. It is what I have seen in the presence of my Father that I tell, and it is what you have heard from your father that you do."

They answered,

"Our father is Abraham."

I said to them,

"If you are Abraham's children, then do what Abraham did. But instead you are trying to kill me, a man who has told you the truth he has heard from God. Abraham would not have done that. You are doing as your father does."

They said to me,

"We are not illegitimate children. We have one father, God himself."

"I said to them,

"If God were your father, you would love me, for I have come from God. I have not come of my own accord, but he has sent me. Why is it that you do not understand what I say? It is because you cannot bear to listen to my message. The devil is the father you are sprung from, and you want to carry out your father's wishes. He was a murderer from the first, and he has nothing to do with the truth, for there is no truth in him. When he tells a lie, he speaks in his true character, for he is a liar and the father of them. But because I tell the truth you will not believe me. Who among you can prove me guilty of sin? But if I tell you the truth, why do you refuse to believe me? Whoever is sprung from God listens to God's words. The reason you refuse to listen is that you are not sprung from God."

The Jews answered,

"Are we not right in saying that you are a Samaritan and are possessed?"

I answered,

"I am not possessed, but I have respect for my Father, and you have no respect for me. But I do not seek honor for myself; there is someone who seeks it for me, and is the judge of it. I tell you, if anyone observes my teaching, he will never experience death."

The Jews said to me,

"Now we are sure that you are possessed! Abraham is dead and so are the prophets, and yet you say, 'If anyone observes my teaching, he will never know what death is!' Are you a greater man than our forefather Abraham? Yet he is dead and the prophets are dead. What do you claim to be?"

I answered,

"If I show special honor to myself, such honor counts for nothing. It is my Father who shows me honor. You say he is your God, yet you have never come to know him. But I know him. If I say I do not know him, I will be a liar like yourselves. No! I do know him, and I am faithful to his message. Your forefather Abraham exulted at the thought of seeing my coming. He has seen it, and it has made him glad."

The Jews said to me,

"You are not fifty years old, and have you seen Abraham?"

I said to them,

"I tell you, I existed before Abraham was born!"

At that, the Jews picked up stones to throw at me, but I disappeared and made my way out of the Temple.

THE MINISTRY IN PEREA

The Mission of the Seventy

I appointed seventy-two others, and sent them on before me, two by two, to every town or place to which I intended to come. And I said to them,

"The harvest is abundant enough, but the reapers are few. So pray to the owner of the harvest to send reapers to gather it. Now go. Here I send you out like lambs among wolves. Carry no purse nor wallet nor shoes, and do not stop to exchange civilities with anyone on the way. Whenever you go to stay at a house, first say, 'Peace to this household!' If there is anyone there who loves peace, your blessing will rest upon him, but if there is not, it will come back to you. Stay at the same house, eating and drinking what they offer you, for the workman deserves his pay. Do not change from one house to another. Whenever you come to a town and they welcome you, eat what is offered you, and cure the sick there, and say to them, 'The

Kingdom of God is close upon you!' But whenever you come to a town and they do not welcome you, go out into the open streets and say, 'The very dust of your town that sticks to our feet we wipe off in protest. But understand this: the Kingdom of God is at hand!' . . . Whoever listens to you listens to me, and whoever disregards you disregards me, and whoever disregards me disregards him who sent me."

The Return of the Seventy

The seventy-two came back delighted, and said,

"Master, when we use your name the very demons submit to us!"

I said to them,

"I saw Satan fall from heaven like a flash of lightning! Here I have given you the power to tread on snakes and scorpions, and to trample on all the power of the enemy. Nothing will hurt you at all. But do not be glad that the spirits submit to you, but be glad that your names are enrolled in heaven."

The Meek and Lowly

At that moment I was inspired with joy, and said,

"I thank you, Father, Lord of heaven and earth, for hiding all this from the learned and intelligent, and revealing it to children! Yes, I thank you, Father, for choosing to have it so! Everything has been handed over to me by my Father, and no one knows who the Son is but the Father, nor who the Father is but the Son, and anyone to whom the Son chooses to reveal him."

And I turned to my disciples when they were alone, and said,

"Blessed are the eyes that see what you see! For I tell you, many prophets and kings have wished to see what you see, and could not see it, and to hear what you hear, and could not hear it!

"Come to me, all of you who toil and are burdened, and I will let you rest. Let my yoke be put upon you, and learn from me, for I am gentle and humble-minded, and your hearts will find rest, for the yoke I offer you is a kindly one, and the load I ask you to bear is light."

The Unrepentant Cities

Then I began to reproach the towns in which my numerous wonders had been done, because they did not repent.

"Alas for you, Chorazin! Alas for you, Bethsaida! For if the wonders that have been done in you had been done in Tyre and Sidon, they would have repented in sackcloth and ashes long ago! But I tell you, Tyre and Sidon will fare better on the Day of Judgment than you will! And you, Capernaum! Are you to be exalted to the skies? You will go down among the dead! For if the wonders that have been done in you had been done in Sodom, it would have stood until today. But I tell you that the land of Sodom will fare better on the Day of Judgment than you will!"

The Good Samaritan

Then an expert in the Law got up to test me and said,
"Master, what must I do to make sure of eternal life?"
I said to him,
"What does the Law say? How does it read?"
He answered,
" 'You must love the Lord your God with your whole heart,

your whole soul, your whole strength, and your whole mind,' and 'your neighbor as you do yourself.' "

I said to him,

"You are right. Do that, and you will live."

But he, wishing to justify his question, said,

"And who is my neighbor?"

I replied,

"A man was on his way down from Jerusalem to Jericho, when he fell into the hands of robbers, and they stripped him and beat him and went off leaving him half dead. Now a priest happened to be going that way, and when he saw him, he went by on the other side of the road. And a Levite also came to the place, and when he saw him, he went by on the other side. But a Samaritan who was traveling that way came upon him, and when he saw him he pitied him, and he went up to him and dressed his wounds with oil and wine and bound them up. And he put him on his own mule and brought him to an inn and took care of him. The next day he took out a dollar and gave it to the innkeeper and said, 'Take care of him, and whatever more you spend I will refund to you on my way back.' Which of these three do you think proved himself a neighbor to the man who fell into the robbers' hands?"

He said,

"The man who took pity on him."

I said to him,

"Go and do so yourself!"

IN JERUSALEM—THE ATTEMPT TO ARREST ME

The Friends at Bethany

As we continued our journey, I came to a certain village, and a woman named Martha welcomed me to her house. She had a sister named Mary, who seated herself at my feet, and listened to what I was saying. But Martha was worried with all she had to do for us, and she came up and said,

"Master, does it make no difference to you that my sister has left me to do all the work alone? Tell her to help me."

I answered,

"Martha, Martha, you are worried and anxious about many things, but our wants are few, indeed there is only one thing we need. For Mary has chosen the right thing, and it must not be taken away from her."

A Miracle in Jerusalem

As I passed along, I saw a man who had been blind from his birth. My disciples asked me,

"Master, for whose sin was this man born blind? For his own, or for that of his parents?"

I answered,

"It was neither for his own sin nor for that of his parents, but to let what God can do be illustrated in his case. We must carry on the work of him who has sent me while the daylight lasts. Night is coming, when no one can do any work. As long as I am in the world, I am a light for the world."

As I said this I spat on the ground and made clay with the saliva, and I put the clay on the man's eyes, and said to him,

"Go and wash them in the Pool of Siloam"—a name which means One who has been sent. So he went and washed them, and went home able to see.

Then his neighbors and people who had formerly seen him begging, said,

"Is not this the man who used to sit and beg?"

Some said,

"Yes! It is he!"

Others said,

"No! but he looks like him."

He himself said,

"I am the man."

So they said to him,

"Then how does it happen that you can see?"

He answered,

"The man they call Jesus made some clay and rubbed it on my eyes, and said to me, 'Go to Siloam and wash them.' So I went and when I had washed them I could see."

They said to him,

"Where is he?"

He answered,

"I do not know."

They took the man who had been blind to the Pharisees. Now it was on the Sabbath that I had made the clay and made him able to see. So once more the Pharisees asked him how he had become able to see, and he said to them,

"He put some clay on my eyes, and I washed them, and I can see."

Then some of the Pharisees said,

"This man does not come from God, for he does not keep the Sabbath."

But others said,

"How can a sinful man show such signs as this?"

And there was a division of opinion among them. So they asked the blind man again,

"What have you to say about him, because he has made you able to see?"

He said,

"He is a prophet!"

But the Jews would not believe that he had been blind and had become able to see until they summoned the parents of the man who had been given his sight, and asked them,

"Is this your son, who you say was born blind? How is it that he can see now?"

His parents answered,

"We know that this is our son, and that he was born blind. But we do not know how it is that he can see now, or who has made him able to see. You must ask him. He is grown up. Let him tell you about himself."

His parents said this because they were afraid of the Jews, for the Jews had already made an agreement that if anyone

[106]

acknowledged me as the Christ, he should be excluded from the synagogues. That was why his parents said, "He is grown up; you must ask him." So they again summoned the man who had been blind, and they said to him,

"Give God the praise. This man we know is a sinful man."

He answered,

"I do not know about his being a sinful man. All I know is that I was blind before and now I can see."

They said to him,

"What did he do to you? How did he make you able to see?"

He answered,

"I have already told you and you would not listen. Why do you want to hear it again? Do you want to become disciples of his too?"

Then they sneered at him, and said,

"You are a disciple of his yourself, but we are disciples of Moses. We know that God spoke to Moses, but we do not know where this man came from."

The man answered,

"There is something very strange about this! You do not know where he came from, and yet he has made me able to see! We know that God does not listen to sinful people, but if a man is devout and obeys God, God will listen to him. It was never heard of in this world that anyone made a man born blind able to see. If this man were not from God, he could not do anything."

They answered,

"You were born in utter sin, and are you trying to teach us?"

So they excluded him from the synagogue,

I learned that they had excluded him, and I found the man and said to him,

"Do you believe in the Son of Man?"

The man answered,

"Who is he, sir? Tell me, so that I may believe in him."

I said to him,

"You have seen him already, and it is he who is now talking to you."

And he said,

"I believe, sir!" and he fell on his knees before me.

[107]

And I said,

"I have come into this world to judge men, that those who cannot see may see, and that those who can see may become blind."

Some Pharisees who were present heard this, and they said to me,

"Then are we blind too?"

I said to them,

"If you were blind, you would be guilty of no sin, but as it is, you say, 'We can see'; so your sin continues.

The Good Shepherd

"I tell you, any man who does not enter the sheepfold by the door, but climbs over at some other place, is a thief and robber. But the man who enters by the door is the shepherd of the flock. The watchman opens the door to him, and the sheep obey his voice, and he calls to his own sheep and leads them out. When he gets his own flock all out, he goes in front of them, and the sheep follow him, because they know his voice. But they will never follow a stranger but will run away from him, because they do not know the voice of strangers."

This was the figure I used in speaking to them, but they did not understand what I meant by it.

So I said again,

"I tell you, I am the door of the sheepfold. All who have come before me are thieves and robbers, but the sheep would not obey them. I am the door. Whoever enters through me will be saved, and will pass in and out and find pasture. A thief comes only to steal and kill and destroy; I have come to let them have life, and to let them have it in abundance. I am the good shepherd. A good shepherd will give his life for his sheep. A hired man who is not a shepherd and does not own the sheep, when he sees a wolf coming, will leave the sheep and run away, and the wolf will carry them off and scatter the flock. For he is only a hired man, and does not care about the sheep. I am the good shepherd. I know my sheep and my sheep know me, just as the Father knows me and I know the Father, and I am giving my life for my sheep. I have other sheep too that do not belong to this fold. I must lead them too, and they will obey my voice, and they will all become one flock, with one shepherd. This is why the Father loves me, because I am giving my life, but giving it to take it back again. No one has taken it from me, but I am giving it of my own accord. I have power to give it, and I have power to take it back again. These are the orders I have received from my Father."

These words caused a fresh division of opinion among the Jews. Many of them said,

"He is possessed and mad! Why do you listen to him?"

Others said,

"These are not the words of a man who is possessed. Can a madman make blind men see?"

At the Feast of Dedication

That was the time of the Rededication Festival at Jerusalem. It was winter time and I was walking up and down inside the Temple, in Solomon's Colonnade. So the Jews gathered around me and said to me,

"How much longer are you going to keep us in suspense? If you are really the Christ, tell us so frankly!"

I answered,

"I have told you so, and you will not believe it. The things I have been doing by my Father's authority are my credentials, but you do not believe it because you do not belong to my sheep. My sheep listen to my voice, and I know them and they follow me, and I give them eternal life, and they shall never be lost, and no one shall tear them out of my hands. What my Father has intrusted to me is of more importance than everything else, and no one can tear anything out of the Father's hands. The Father and I are one."

The Jews again picked up stones to stone me with. I answered,

"I have let you see many good things from the Father; which of them do you mean to stone me for?"

The Jews answered,

"We are not stoning you for doing anything good, but for your impious talk, and because you, a mere man, make yourself out to be God."

I answered,

"Is it not declared in your Law, 'I said, "You are gods" '? If those to whom God's message was addressed were called gods—and the Scripture cannot be set aside—do you mean to say to me whom the Father has consecrated and made his messenger to the world, 'You are blasphemous,' because I said, 'I am God's Son'? If I am not doing the things my Father does, do not believe me. But if I am doing them, then even if you will not believe me, believe the things I do, in order that you may realize and learn that the Father is in union with me, and I am in union with the Father."

RENEWED MINISTRY IN PEREA

The Pharisees

In consequence of this they again tried to arrest me, and I withdrew out of their reach.

I went across the Jordan again to the place where John used to baptize at first, and there I stayed. And people came to me in great numbers, and they said of me,

"John did not show any sign in proof of his mission, but all that he said about this man was true."

And many became believers in me in that place.

A Pharisee asked me to lunch with him, and I went to his house and took my place at table. The Pharisee noticed that I did not wash before the meal, and he was surprised. But I said to him,

"You Pharisees clean the outside of cups and dishes, but inside you are full of greed and wickedness. You fools! Did not the Creator of the outside make the inside too? But give your inmost life as charity, and you will immediately find everything clean."

After I left the house, the scribes and the Pharisees began to watch me closely and to try to draw me out on many subjects, plotting to entrap me in something I might say.

Meanwhile as the people gathered in thousands, until they actually trod on one another, I proceeded to say to my disciples first of all,

"Beware of the yeast of the Pharisees, that is hypocrisy. There is nothing covered up that is not going to be uncovered, nor secret that is not going to be known."

Warning against Covetousness

Someone in the crowd said to me,

"Master, tell my brother to give me my share of our inheritance."

But I said to him,

"Who made me a judge or arbitrator of your affairs?"

And I said to them,

"Take care! You must be on your guard against any form of greed, for a man's life does not belong to him, no matter how rich he is."

And I told them this story:

"A certain rich man's lands yielded heavily. And he said to himself, 'What am I going to do, for I have nowhere to store my crops?' Then he said, 'This is what I will do; I will tear down my barns and build larger ones, and in them I will store all my grain and my goods. And I will say to my soul, "Soul, you have great wealth stored up for years to come. Now take your ease, eat, drink, and enjoy yourself." ' But God said to him, 'You fool! This very night your soul will be demanded of you. Then who will have all you have prepared?' That is the way with the man who lays up money for himself, and is not rich with God.' "

The Fall of the Tower

Just then some people came up to bring me word of the Galileans whose blood Pilate had mingled with that of their sacrifices. And I answered,

"Do you think, because this happened to them, that these Galileans were worse sinners than any other Galileans? No, I tell you; unless you repent, you will all perish as they did! Or those eighteen people at Siloam who were killed when the tower fell upon them—do you think they were worse offenders than all the other people who live in Jerusalem? No, I tell you; unless you repent, you will all perish as they did!"

I used this figure:

"A man had a fig tree growing in his garden, and he went to look for fruit on it, and could not find any. And he said to the gardener, 'Here I have come three years to look for fruit on this fig tree, without finding any. Cut it down. Why should it waste the ground?' He answered, 'Let it stand this one year more, sir, till I dig around it and manure it; perhaps it will bear fruit next year. But if it does not, you can have it cut down.' "

The Uses of the Sabbath

One Sabbath I was teaching in one of the synagogues, and there was a woman there who for eighteen years had had a sickness caused by a spirit. She was bent double and could not straighten herself up at all. When I saw her I called to her,

"You are freed from your sickness!"

And I laid my hands on her, and she instantly became erect, and praised God. But the leader of the synagogue, in his vexation because I had cured her on the Sabbath, spoke out and said to the crowd,

"There are six days on which it is right to work. Come on them and be cured, but not on the Sabbath day."

But I answered,

"You hypocrites! Does not every one of you untie his ox or his donkey from the stall on the Sabbath and lead him away to water him? And did not this woman, who is a descendant of Abraham, whom Satan has kept bound for eighteen years, have to be released from those bonds on the Sabbath day?"

When I said this, all my opponents were humiliated, and all the people were delighted at all the splendid things that they had seen me do.

A Question of Salvation

So I went about among the towns and villages, teaching and making my way toward Jerusalem. And someone said to me,

"Are only a few to be saved, Master?"

I said to them,

"You must strain every nerve to get in through the narrow door, for I tell you many will try to get in, and will not succeed, when the master of the house gets up and shuts the door, and you begin to stand outside and to knock on the door, and say, 'Open it for us, sir! Then he will answer you and say, 'I do not know where you come from.' Then you will go on to say, 'We have been entertained with you, and you have taught in our streets!' And he will say to you, 'I do not know where you come from. Get away from me, all you wrongdoers!' There you will weep and gnash your teeth when you see Abraham and Isaac and Jacob and all the prophets in the Kingdom of God, while you are put outside. People will come from the east and west and the north and south, and take their

[113]

places in the Kingdom of God. There are those now last who will then be first, and there are those now first who will be last."

A Message to Herod

Just then some Pharisees came up and said to me,
"Go! Get away from here, for Herod wants to kill you!"
I said to them,
"Go and say to that fox, 'Here I am, driving out demons and performing cures, today and tomorrow, and on the third day I will be through. But I must go on today and tomorrow and the next day, for it is not right for a prophet to die outside Jerusalem.' "

The Ox in the Pit

One Sabbath, when I went to take a meal at the house of a member of the council who was a Pharisee, they were watching me closely. There was a man in front of me who had dropsy. And I said to the Pharisees and the experts in the Law,
"Is it right to cure people on the Sabbath or not?"
But they made no answer. And I took hold of the man and cured him and sent him away. Then I said to them,
"Who among you, if his child or his ox falls into a well, will not pull him out at once on the Sabbath?" And they could make no reply to this.

The Chief Place at the Feast

I noticed that the guests picked out the best places, and I gave them this illustration:

"When someone invites you to a wedding supper, do not take the best place, for someone more distinguished than you are may have been invited, and your host will come and say to you, 'Make room for this man,' and then you will proceed in confusion to take the poorest place. But when you are invited anywhere, go and take the poorest place, so that when your host comes in, he will say to you, 'My friend, come to a better place.' So you will be shown consideration before all the other guests. For everyone who exalts himself will be humbled, but the man who humbles himself will be exalted."

And I said to the man who had invited me,

When you give a luncheon or a dinner, do not invite your friends or your brothers or your relatives or your rich neighbors, for then they will invite you in return and you will be repaid. But when you give an entertainment, invite people who are poor, maimed, lame, or blind. Then you will be blessed, because they cannot repay you; for you will be repaid at the resurrection of the upright."

The Slightest Invitation

One of the other guests heard this, and said to me,

"Blessed is the man who shall be at the banquet in the Kingdom of God!"

I said to him,

"A man once gave a great dinner, and invited a large number to it, and when the dinner hour came, he sent around his slave, to say to those who were invited, 'Come! for it is now

[115]

ready!' And they all immediately began to excuse themselves. The first one said to him, 'I have bought a piece of land, and I must go and look at it. Please have me excused.' Another said, 'I have bought five yoke of oxen, and I am going to examine them. Please have me excused.' Another said, 'I have married, and so I cannot come.' So the slave went back, and reported this to his master. Then the master of the house was angry and said to his slave, 'Hurry out into the streets and squares of the city, and bring the poor, the maimed, the blind, and the lame in here!' And the slave said, 'What you ordered, sir, has been done, and there is still room.' And the master said to the slave, 'Go out on the roads and among the hedges, and make them come in, so that my house may be full. For I tell you that none of those men who were invited shall have any of my dinner!' "

Counting the Cost

There were great crowds accompanying me, and once I turned and said to them,

"If anyone comes to me without hating his own father and mother and wife and children and brothers and sisters, and his very life too, he cannot be a disciple of mine. For no one who does not take up his own cross and come after me can be a disciple of mine. What man among you if he wishes to build a tower does not first sit down and estimate the cost of it, to see whether he has enough to complete it? Or else when he has laid his foundation and cannot finish the building, everyone who sees it will begin to ridicule him, and say, 'This man started to erect a building, and could not finish it!' Or what king, if he is going to meet another king in battle, does not sit down first and consider whether he is able with ten thousand men to meet the other who is coming against him with twenty thousand? And if he cannot, while the other is still far away, he sends envoys to him and asks on what terms he will make peace. In just that way, no one of you who does not say goodbye to all he has can be a disciple of mine. Salt is good; but if salt loses its strength, what can it be seasoned with? It is fit neither for the ground nor the manure heap; people throw it away. Let him who has ears to hear with, listen!"

The Ninety and Nine

All the tax-collectors and irreligious people were crowding up to hear me. And the Pharisees and scribes grumbled, and said,

"This man welcomes irreligious people, and even eats with them!"

So in speaking to them I used this figure:

"What man among you, if he has a hundred sheep, and loses one of them, does not leave the ninety-nine in the wilderness, and go in search of the one that is lost, until he finds it? And when he finds it, he puts it on his shoulders with joy, and when he reaches home, he calls in his friends and neighbors, and says to them, 'Congratulate me, for I have found my lost sheep!' I tell you, in just that way there will be more joy in heaven over one sinful person who repents, than over ninety-nine upright people who do not need any repentance.

The Lost Coin

"Or what woman who has ten silver coins and loses one, does not light the lamp and sweep the house and look carefully until she finds it? And when she finds it, she calls in her friends and neighbors, and says to them, 'Congratulate me, for I have found the coin that I lost!' In just that way, I tell you, there is joy among the angels of God over one sinful person who repents!"

The Prodigal Son

And I said,

"A man had two sons. The younger of them said to his father, 'Father, give me my share of the property.' So he divided his property between them. Not many days later, the younger son gathered up all he had, and went away to a distant country, and there he squandered his property by fast living. After he had spent it all, a severe famine arose in that country, and he began to be in want. And he went and hired himself out to a resident of the country, and he sent him into his fields to tend pigs. And he was ready to fill himself with the pods the pigs were eating, and no one would give him anything. When he came to himself he said, 'How many hired men my father has, who have more than enough to eat, and here I am, dying of hunger! I will get up, and go to my father, and say to him, "Father, I have sinned against heaven and in your eyes; I no longer deserve to be called your son; treat me like one of your hired men!"' And he got up and went to his father. But while he was still a long way off, his father saw him, and pitied him, and ran and fell on his neck, and kissed him. His son said to him, 'Father, I have sinned against heaven, and in your eyes; I no longer deserve to be called your son; treat me like one of your hired men!' But his father said to his slave, 'Make haste and get out the best robe, and put it on him, and put a ring on his hand, and shoes on his feet; and get the calf we are fattening, and kill it, and let us feast and celebrate, for my son here was dead, and he has come to life; he was lost, and he is found!' So they began to celebrate. But his elder son was in the field. When he came in and approached the house, he heard music and dancing, and he called one of the servants to him and asked him what it meant. He said to him, 'Your brother has come, and your father has killed the calf he has been fattening, because he has gotten him back alive and well.' But he was angry, and would not go into the house. And his father came out and urged him. And he said to his father, 'Here I have served you all these years, and have never disobeyed an order of yours, and you have never given me a kid, so that I could entertain my friends. But when your son came here, who has eaten up your property with women of the streets, for him you killed the calf you have been fattening!' But he said to him, 'My child, you have been with me all the time, and everything I have is yours. But we had to celebrate and be glad, because your brother was dead, and has come to life, and was lost and is found!' "

The Unjust Steward

And I said to my disciples,
"There was a rich man who had a manager, and it was reported to him that this man was squandering his property. So he called him in and said to him, 'What is this that I hear about you? Make an accounting for your conduct of my affairs, for you cannot be manager any longer!' Then the manager said to himself, 'What am I going to do, because my master is going to take my position away from me? I cannot dig; I am ashamed to beg. I know what I will do, so that when I am removed from my position people will take me into their homes.' Then he called in each of his master's debtors, and he said to the first one, 'How much do you owe my master?' He said, 'Eight hundred gallons of oil.' And he said to him, 'Here is your agreement; sit down and write four hundred!' Then he said to another, 'And how much do you owe?' He answered, 'Fifteen hundred bushels of wheat.' He said to him, 'Here is your agreement; write twelve hundred.' And his master praised the dishonest manager, because he had acted shrewdly. For the sons of this age are shrewder in their relation to their own age than the sons of the light. So I tell you, make friends for yourselves with your ill-gotten wealth, so that when it fails, they may take you into the eternal dwellings. The man who can be trusted in a very small matter

can be trusted in a large one, and the man who cannot be trusted in a very small matter cannot be trusted in a large one. So if you have proved untrustworthy in using your ill-gotten wealth, who will trust you with true riches? And if you have been untrustworthy about what belonged to someone else, who will give you what belongs to you? No servant can belong to two masters, for he will either hate one and love the other, or he will stand by one and make light of the other. You cannot serve God and money!"

A Parable to the Lovers of Money

The Pharisees, who were avaricious, heard all this, and they ridiculed me. And I said to them,

"You are the men who parade your uprightness before people, but God knows your hearts. For what men consider great is detestable in the sight of God. Until John came, it was the Law and the Prophets. From that time the Kingdom of God has been proclaimed, and everyone has been crowding into it. But it is easier for heaven and earth to pass away than for one dotting of an *i* in the Law to go unfulfilled. Anyone who divorces his wife and marries another woman commits adultery, and whoever marries a woman who has been divorced from her husband commits adultery.

"There was once a rich man, who used to dress in purple and fine linen, and to live in luxury every day. And a beggar named Lazarus was put down at his gate covered with sores and eager to satisfy his hunger with what was thrown away from the rich man's table. Why, the very dogs came and licked his sores. And it came about that the beggar died and was carried away by the angels to the companionship of Abraham, and the rich man too died and was buried. And in Hades he looked up, tormented as he was, and saw Abraham far away, with Lazarus beside him. And he called to him and said, 'Father Abraham! take pity on me, and send Lazarus to dip the tip of his finger in water and cool my tongue, for I am in torment, here in the flames!' And Abraham said, 'My child, remember that you received your blessings in your lifetime, and Lazarus had his misfortunes in his; and now he is being comforted here, while you are in anguish. Besides there is a great chasm set between you and us, so that those who want to go over from this side to you cannot, and they cannot cross from your side to us.' And he said, 'Then I beg you, father, to send him to my father's house, for I have five brothers; let him warn them so that they will not also come to this place of torture.' Abraham answered, 'They have Moses and the prophets; let them listen to them.' But he said, 'No! Father Abraham, but if someone will go to them from the dead, they will repent!' He answered, 'If they will not listen to Moses and the prophets, they will not be convinced even if someone rises from the dead!' "

"Increase our Faith"

The apostles said to me,
"Give us more faith."
And I said,
"If your faith is as big as a mustard seed, you might have said to this mulberry tree, 'Be pulled up by the roots and planted in the sea,' and it would have obeyed you!

"What man among you, if he has a servant ploughing or keeping sheep, will say to him when he comes in from the field, 'Come at once and sit down at the table,' instead of saying to him, 'Get my supper ready, and dress yourself, and wait on me while I eat and drink, and you can eat and drink afterward'? Is he grateful to the slave for doing what he has been ordered to do? So you also, when you do all you have been ordered to do, must say, 'We are good-for-nothing slaves! We have done only what we ought to have done!' "

NEAR JERUSALEM—THE PLOT TO KILL ME

The Raising of Lazarus

Now my friend Lazarus was sick; he lived in Bethany, the village of Mary and her sister Martha. It was the Mary who poured perfume upon me and wiped my feet with her hair, whose brother Lazarus was sick. So the sisters sent this message to me: "Master, your friend is sick." When I received it I said,

"This sickness is not to end in death, but is for the honor of God, that through it the Son of God may be honored."

I loved Martha and her sister and Lazarus. So when I heard that Lazarus was sick, I stayed on for two days in the place where I was, and then afterward said to my disciples,

"Let us go back to Judea."

The disciples said to me,

"Master, the Jews have just been trying to stone you, and are you going back there again?"

I answered,

"Is not the day twelve hours long? If a man travels by day he will not stumble, for he can see the light of his world; but if he travels at night he will stumble because he has no light."

I told them this, and then I added,

"Our friend Lazarus has fallen asleep, but I am going there to wake him."

The disciples said to me,

"Master, if he has fallen asleep he will recover."

Now I had referred to his death. But they supposed that I meant a natural falling asleep. So I then told them plainly,

"Lazarus is dead, and for your sake I am glad that I was not there, so that you may learn to believe in me. But let us go to him."

So Thomas the Twin said to his fellow-disciples,
"Let us go also, and die with him."

When I arrived I found that Lazarus had been buried for four days. Now Bethany is only about two miles from Jerusalem, and a number of Jews had come out to see Mary and Martha, to condole with them about their brother. When Martha heard that I was coming she came out to meet me, but Mary remained at home. Martha said to me,

"Master, if you had been here, my brother would not have died! Even now I know that anything you ask God for, he will give you."

I said to her,

"Your brother will rise."

Martha said to me,

"I know that he will rise at the resurrection, on the Last Day."

I said to her,

"I myself am Resurrection and Life. He who believes in me will live on, even if he dies, and no one who is alive and believes in me will ever die. Do you believe that?"

She said to me,

"Yes, Master, I do indeed believe that you are the Christ, the Son of God, who was to come into the world."

With these words she went and called her sister Mary, whispering to her,

"Here is the Master, asking for you."

When she heard it she sprang up and came to me, for I had not yet come into the village, but was still at the place where Martha had met me. The Jews who were sitting with her in the house, condoling with her, when they saw Mary spring up and go out, supposed that she was going to weep at the tomb, and followed her. When Mary came where I was and saw me, she fell at my feet, and said,

"Master, if you had been here, my brother would not have died!"

When I saw her weep and the Jews who had come with her weeping too, repressing a groan, and yet showing great agitation, I said,

"Where have you laid him?"

[123]

They answered,

"Come and see, Master."

I shed tears. So the Jews said,

"See how much he loved him!"

But some of them said,

"Could not this man, who opened the eyes of that blind man, have kept Lazarus from dying?"

Again repressing a groan, I went to the tomb. It was a cave with a stone laid against the mouth of it. I said,

"Move the stone away."

The dead man's sister, Martha, said to me,

"Master, by this time he is decaying, for he has been dead four days."

I said to her,

"Have I not promised you that if you will believe in me you will see the glory of God?"

So they moved the stone away. And I looked upward and said,

"Father, I thank you for listening to me, though I knew that you always listen to me. But I have said this for the sake of the people that are standing around me that they may believe that you have made me your messenger."

After saying this I called out in a loud voice,

"Lazarus, come out!"

The dead man came out, bound hand and foot with wrappings, and with his face muffled with a handkerchief. I said to them,

"Unbind him and let him move."

So it came about that many of the Jews who had come to visit Mary and saw what I did, came to believe in me, but some of them went back to the Pharisees and told them what I had done.

Then the high priests and the Pharisees called a meeting of the council, and they said,

"What are we to do about the fact that this man is showing so many signs? If we let him go on, everybody will believe in him, and then the Romans will come and put an end to our holy place and our people."

But one of them, Caiaphas, who was high priest that year, said to them,

"You know nothing about it. You do not realize that it is to your interest that one man should die for the people, instead of the whole nation being destroyed."

Now he was not self-moved in saying this, but as high priest for that year he was inspired to say that I was to die for the nation—and not only for the nation but also for the purpose of uniting the scattered children of God. So from that day they planned to kill me.

WITHDRAWAL TO EPHRAIM

In consequence of this, I did not appear in public among the Jews any longer, but I left that neighborhood and went to the district near the desert, to a town called Ephraim, and stayed there with my disciples.

The Coming of the Kingdom

I was asked by the Pharisees when the Kingdom of God would come, and I answered,

"The Kingdom of God is not coming visibly, and people will not say, 'Look! Here it is!' or 'There it is!' for the Kingdom of God is within you."

And I said to my disciples,

"The time will come when you will long to see one of the days of the Son of Man, and you will not be able to do so. Men will say to you, 'Look! There he is!' or, 'Look! Here he is!' Do not go off in pursuit of him, for just as when the lightning flashes, it shines from one end of the sky to the other, that will be the way with the Son of Man. But first he must go through much suffering, and be refused by this age. In the time of the Son of Man it will be just as it was in the time of Noah. People went on eating, drinking, marrying, and being married up to the very day that Noah got into the ark and the flood came and destroyed them all. Or as it was in Lot's time; they went on eating, drinking, buying, selling, planting, and building, but the day Lot left Sodom, it rained fire and brimstone from heaven and destroyed them all. It will be like that on the day when the Son of Man appears. A man who is on the roof of his house that day, with his goods in the house, must not go down to get them, and a man in the field, too, must not turn back. Remember Lot's wife. Whoever tries to preserve his life will lose it, and whoever loses his life will preserve it."

The Unjust Judge

I gave them an illustration to show that they must always pray and not give up, and I said,

"There was once in a city a judge who had no fear of God and no respect for men. There was a widow in the city and she came to him and said, 'Protect me from my opponent.' And he would not for a time, but afterward he said to himself, 'Though I have no fear of God nor respect for men, yet because this widow bothers me, I will protect her, so that she may not finally wear me out with her coming.'"

And said,

"Listen to what this dishonest judge said! Then will not God provide protection for his chosen people, who cry out to him day and night? I tell you, he will make haste to provide it! But when the Son of Man comes, will he find faith on earth?"

The Pharisee and the Publican

To some who were confident of their own uprightness, and thought nothing of others, I used this illustration:

"Two men went up to the Temple to pray; one was a Pharisee and the other a tax-collector. The Pharisee stood up and uttered this prayer to himself: 'O God, I thank you that I am not like other men, greedy, dishonest, or adulterous, like that tax-collector. I fast two days in the week; I pay tithes on everything I get.' But the tax-collector stood at a distance and would not even raise his eyes to heaven, but struck his breast, and said, 'O God, have mercy on a sinner like me!' I tell you, it was he who went back to his house with God's approval, and not the other. For everyone who exalts himself will be humbled, but the man who humbles himself will be exalted."

And some Pharisees came up to me to test me, and they said,

"Is it right for a man to divorce his wife for any cause?"

But I answered,

"Did you never read that the Creator at the beginning made them male and female, and said, 'For this reason a man shall leave his father and mother and be united to his wife, and the two of them shall become one'? So they are no longer two but one. Therefore, what God has joined together, man must not try to separate."

They said to me,

"Then why did Moses command us to draw up a written divorce-notice and give it to her?"

I said to them,

"It was on account of your perversity that Moses permitted you to divorce your wives, but it was not so at the beginning. I tell you that whoever divorces his wife on any ground but her unfaithfulness, and marries another woman, commits adultery."

The disciples said to me,

"If that is a man's relation to his wife, it is better not to marry!"

I said to them,

"It is not everyone who can accept that, but only those who have a special gift. For some are incapable of marriage from their birth, and some have been made so by men, and some have made themselves so for the sake of the Kingdom of Heaven. Let him accept it who can."

Then some children were brought up to me so that I might lay my hands on them and pray, but my disciples reproved the people for it. When I saw it, I was indignant, and said to them,

"Let the children come to me; do not try to stop them, for the Kingdom of God belongs to such as they. I tell you, who-

ever does not accept the Kingdom of God like a child shall
not enter it at all."

And I took the children in my arms and laid my hands on
them and blessed them.

The Rich Young Ruler

As I was starting again on my journey, a man came running
up to me, and knelt at my feet and asked me,

"Master, what good deed must I do to obtain eternal life?"

But I said to him,

"Why do you ask me about what is good? There is only one
who is good. But if you want to enter that life, keep the
commandments."

He said to me,

"Which ones?"

I said,

"These: 'You shall not murder, You shall not commit
adultery, You shall not steal, You shall not bear false witness,
Honor your father and mother,' and 'You shall love your
neighbor as you do yourself.' "

The young man said to me,

"I have obeyed all these commandments. What do I still
lack?"

And I looked at him and loved him, and said to him,

"There is one thing that you lack. If you want to be perfect,
go! Sell your property and give the money to the poor, and
you will have riches in heaven. Then come back and be a
follower of mine."

But when the young man heard my words, he went away
much cast down, for he had a great deal of property.

I said to my disciples,

"I tell you, it will be hard for a rich man to get into the
Kingdom of Heaven!"

The disciples were amazed at what I said. And I said to
them again,

"My children, how hard it is to enter the Kingdom of God! It is easier for a camel to get through the eye of a needle than for a rich man to get into the Kingdom of God!"

The Blind Man of Jericho

And we came to Jericho. As I was leaving the town with my disciples and a great crowd, Timaeus' son Bartimaeus, a blind beggar, was sitting at the roadside. When he heard that it was I, he began to cry out,

"Jesus, you son of David, take pity on me!"

Many of the people rebuked him and told him to be still. But he cried out all the louder,

"You son of David, take pity on me!"

I stopped and said,

"Call him here."

And they called the blind man and said to him,

"Courage now! Get up, he is calling you!"

And he threw off his coat and sprang to his feet and came up to me. I spoke to him and said,

"What do you want me to do for you?"

The blind man said to me,

"Master, let me regain my sight!"

I said to him,

"Go your way. Your faith has cured you."

And he immediately regained his sight and followed me along the road.

The Visit to Zaccheus

And I went into Jericho and was passing through it. Now there was a man named Zaccheus, the principal tax-collector, a rich man, who wanted to see who I was, and he could not because of the crowd, for he was a small man. So he ran on ahead and climbed up into a sycamore tree, to see me, for I was coming that way. When I reached the place, I looked up and said to him,

"Zaccheus, come down quickly! for I must stay at your house today."

And he came down quickly and welcomed me gladly. And when they saw this, everyone complained, and said,

"He has gone to stay with an irreligious man!"

But Zaccheus stopped and said to me,

"See, Master! I will give half my property to the poor, and if I have defrauded anyone of anything, I will pay him four times as much."

I said to him,

"Salvation has come to this house today, for he too is a descendant of Abraham. For the Son of Man has come to search for what was lost and to save it."

The Parable of the Pounds

As they were listening to this, I went on to give them an illustration, because I was near Jerusalem and they supposed that the Kingdom of God was immediately going to appear. So I said,

"A nobleman once went to a distant country to secure his appointment to a kingdom and then return. And he called in ten of his slaves and gave them each twenty dollars and told them to trade with it while he was gone. But his countrymen hated him, and they sent a delegation after him to say, 'We do not want this man made king over us.' And when he had secured the appointment and returned, he ordered the slaves to whom he had given the money to be called in, so that he could find out how much they had made. The first one came in and said, 'Your twenty dollars has made two hundred, sir!' "

And he said to him, 'Well done, my excellent slave! You have proved trustworthy about a very small amount, you shall be governor of ten towns.' The second came in and said, 'Your twenty dollars has made a hundred, sir!' " And he said to him, 'And you shall be governor of five towns!' And the other one came in and said, 'Here is your twenty dollars, sir. I have kept it put away in a handkerchief, for I was afraid of you, for you are a stern man. You pick up what you did not lay down, and reap what you did not sow.' He said to him, 'Out of your own mouth I will convict you, you wretched slave! You knew, did you, that I was a stern man, and that I pick up what I did not lay down, and harvest what I did not sow? Then why did you not put my money in the bank, so that when I came back I could have gotten it with interest?' And he said to the by-standers, 'Take the twenty dollars away from him, and give it to the man who has the two hundred!' They said to him, 'He has two hundred, sir!'— 'I tell you, the man who has will have more given him, and from the man who has nothing, even what he has will be taken away! But bring those enemies of mine here who did not want me made king over them, and slaughter them in my presence!' "

With these words I went on ahead of them, on my way to Jerusalem.

Going up to Jerusalem

Now the Jewish Passover Festival was approaching and many people went up to Jerusalem from the country, to purify themselves before the Passover. So they were looking for me there, and asking one another as they stood in the Temple,

"What do you think? Do you think he will not come to the festival at all?"

For the high priests and the Pharisees had given orders that anyone who found out where I was should let them know, so that they might arrest me.

The Feast at Bethany

Six days before the Passover I came to Bethany, where Lazarus, whom I had raised from the dead, was living. They gave a dinner for me there, and Martha waited on us, while Lazarus was at the table with me. And Mary took a pound of choice perfume, very costly, and poured it on my feet, and then wiped my feet with her hair, and the whole house was filled with the fragrance of the perfume. But Judas Iscariot, one of my disciples, who was going to betray me, said,

"Why was this perfume not sold for sixty dollars, and the money given to the poor?"

But he did not say this because he cared about the poor, but because he was a thief and when he had charge of the purse he used to take what was put in it. I said,

"Let her alone; let her keep it for the day of my funeral, for you always have the poor among you, but you will not always have me. I tell you, wherever the good news is preached all over the world, what she has done will also be told, in memory of her."

A great many of the Jews found out that I was there, and they came to Bethany not only to see me but also to see Lazarus, whom I had raised from the dead. But the high priests planned to kill Lazarus also, for because of him many of the Jews were leaving them and becoming believers in me.

THE LAST WEEK
PALM SUNDAY—THE DAY OF TRIUMPH

The Triumphant Entry

When we were getting near Jerusalem, and had come to Bethphage and Bethany near the Mount of Olives, I sent two of my disciples on ahead, and said to them,

"Go to the village that lies in front of you, and as soon as you enter it you will find tied there a colt that has never been ridden. Untie it and bring it here. And if anybody says to you, 'Why are you doing that?' say, 'The Master needs it, and will send it back here directly.' "

Now this happened in fulfilment of what was said by the prophet,

> "Tell the daughter of Zion,
> 'Here is your king coming to you,
> Gentle, and riding on an ass,
> And on the foal of a beast of burden.' "

And they set off and found a colt tied in the street at the door of a house, and they untied it. Some of the bystanders said to them,

"What are you doing, untying the colt?"

But they answered them as I had told them to do, and the men let them take it. So they brought the colt to me, and they threw their coats over it and I mounted it. And many of the people spread their coats in the road, and others cut straw from the fields and scattered it in my path.

Just as I was coming down the Mount of Olives and approaching the city, the whole throng of my disciples began to praise God loudly and joyfully, for all the wonders they had

[134]

seen. And the crowds that went in front of me and that followed me shouted,

"God bless the Son of David!
Blessed be he who comes in the Lord's name.
God bless him from on high!
Blessed be the reign of our father David which is coming!"

My disciples did not understand this at the time but after I was glorified they remembered that this was said of me in Scripture and that it had happened to me. The crowd that had been with me when I called Lazarus out of the tomb and raised him from the dead was telling about it. That was why the crowd came out to meet me, because they heard that I had showed that sign.

Some Pharisees in the crowd said to me,
"Master, reprove your disciples!"
And I answered,
"I tell you, if they keep silence, the stones will cry out!"
As I approached the city and saw it, I wept over it, and said,
"If you yourself only knew today the conditions of peace! But as it is, they are hidden from you. For a time is coming upon you when your enemies will throw up earthworks about you and surround you and shut you in on all sides, and they will throw you and your children within you to the ground, and they will not leave one stone upon another within you because you did not know when God visited you!"
When I came into Jerusalem, the whole city was stirred, and everyone asked,
"Who is he?"
The crowd answered,
"It is Jesus, the prophet of Nazareth in Galilee!"
So the Pharisees said to one another,
"You see, you cannot do anything! The whole world has run after him!"
And I came into Jerusalem and into the Temple, and looked it all over; then, as it was already late, I went out with the Twelve to Bethany.

The Cursing of the Fig Tree

On the next day, after we had left Bethany, I felt hungry. And I saw in the distance a fig tree covered with leaves, and I went up to it to see if I could find any figs on it. When I reached it I found nothing but leaves, for it was not the time for figs. And I spoke to the tree and said to it,

"May no one ever eat fruit from you any more!"

And my disciples heard it.

The Cleansing of the Temple

When we reached Jerusalem, I went into the Temple, and began to drive out of it those who were buying or selling things in it, and I upset the money-changers' tables and the pigeon-dealers' seats, and I would not allow anyone to carry anything through the Temple. And I taught them, and said,

"Does not the Scripture say, 'My house shall be called a house of prayer for all the nations'? But you have made it a robbers' cave."

And blind and lame people came up to me in the Temple, and I cured them. But when the high priests and the scribes saw the wonders that I did and saw the boys shouting in the Temple, "God bless the Son of David!" they were indignant, and said to me,

"Do you hear what they are saying?"

I said to them,

"Yes. Did you never read, 'You have drawn praise from the mouths of children and infants'?"

The high priests and scribes and the leading men of the people were trying to destroy me, but they could not find any way to do it, for all the people hung upon my words.

And I left them, and went out of the city to Bethany, and spent the night there.

TUESDAY—THE DAY OF CONTROVERSY

The Lesson from the Withered Fig Tree

In the morning as we were passing along, we saw that the fig tree was withered, to its very roots. And Peter remembered about it and said to me,

"Look, Master! The fig tree that you cursed is withered up!"

I answered and said to them,

"Have faith in God! I tell you, whoever says to this mountain, 'Get up and throw yourself into the sea!' and has no doubt in his mind, but his faith that what he says will happen, shall have it. Therefore I tell you, whenever you pray or ask for anything, have faith that it has been granted you, and you shall have it. And whenever you stand up to pray, if you have a grievance against anyone, forgive him, so that your Father in heaven too may forgive you your offenses."

The Challenge of My Authority

When I had entered the Temple, and was teaching, the high priests and the elders of the people came up to me, and said,

"What authority have you for doing as you do, and who gave you this authority?"

I answered,

"Let me ask you one question, and if you answer it, I will tell you what authority I have for doing as I do. Where did

'John's baptism come from? Was it from heaven, or from men?"

And they argued with one another,

"If we say, 'It was from heaven,' he will say to us, 'Then why did you not believe him?' But if we say, 'From men,' we have the people to fear, for they all consider John a prophet."

And they answered me,

"We do not know."

I said to them,

"Nor will I tell you what authority I have for doing as I do.

THREE WARNING PARABLES

The Two Sons

"But what do you think? There was a man who had two sons. He went to the first and said, 'My son, go and work in the vineyard today.' And he answered, 'I will, sir,' but he did not go. Then the man went to the second son, and told him the same thing. And he answered 'I will not!' But afterward he changed his mind and went. Which of the two did what his father wanted?"

They said,

"The second one."

I said to them,

"I tell you, the tax-collectors and prostitutes are going into the Kingdom of God ahead of you. For John came to you with a way of uprightness, and you would not believe him. The tax-collectors and prostitutes believed him, but even after seeing that, you would not change your minds and believe him!

The Wicked Husbandman

"Listen to another figure. There was a land owner who planted a vineyard and fenced it in, and hewed out a wine-vat in it, and built a watch-tower, and leased it to tenants, and left the neighborhood. When the time for the vintage approached he sent his slaves to the tenants to receive his share. But the tenants took his slaves and beat one and killed another and stoned a third. Again he sent other slaves and more of them than he had sent at first, and they treated them in the same way. Finally he sent his son to them, thinking, 'They will respect my son.' But when the tenants saw his son, they said to one another, 'This is his heir! Come on, let us kill him, and get his inheritance!' So they took him and drove him out of the vineyard and killed him. When the owner of the vineyard comes back, therefore, what will he do to these tenants?"

They said to me,

"He will put the wretches to a miserable death, and let the vineyard to other tenants who will give him his share of the vintage when it is due."

I said to them,

"Did you never read in the Scriptures,

> " 'That stone which the builders rejected
> Has become the cornerstone;
> This came from the Lord,
> And seems marvelous to us'?

"That, I tell you, is why the Kingdom of God will be taken away from you, and given to a people that will produce its proper fruit. Whoever falls on that stone will be shattered, but whoever it falls upon will be pulverized."

When the high priests and the Pharisees heard my figures, they knew that I was speaking about them, and they wanted to have me arrested, but they were afraid of the people, for the people considered me a prophet.

The Marriage of the King's Son

And I spoke to them again in figures, and said,

"The Kingdom of Heaven is like a king, who gave a wedding banquet for his son. And he sent his slaves to summon those who had been invited to the banquet, and they would not come. He sent other slaves a second time, and said to them, 'Tell those who have been asked, "Here I have my banquet all ready. Come to the banquet!"' But they took no notice of it, and went off, one to his estate, and another to his business, and the rest seized his slaves, and ill treated them and killed them. This made the king angry, and he sent his troops and put those murderers to death and burned their city. Then he said to his slaves, 'The banquet is ready, but those who were invited have proved unworthy of it. So go out where the roads leave the city and invite everyone you find to the banquet.' So his slaves went out on the roads, and got together all the people they could find, good or bad, and the hall was filled with guests. But when the king came in to view the guests, he saw among them a man who did not have on wedding clothes. And he said to him, 'My friend, how did you happen to come here without wedding clothes?' But he had nothing to say. Then the king said to his attendants, 'Bind him hand and foot and throw him out into the darkness, there to weep and grind his teeth.' For many are invited but few chosen."

THREE HOSTILE QUESTIONS ASKED OF ME

Tribute to Caesar

Then the Pharisees went and made a plot to entrap me in argument, so they might deliver me unto the power and authority of the governor. So they sent their disciples to me with the Herodians, to say to me,

"Master, we know that you tell the truth, and teach the way of God with sincerity, regardless of the consequences, for you are impartial. So give us your opinion: Is it right to pay the poll-tax to the emperor, or not?"

But I saw their malice, and said,

"Why do you put me to such a test, you hypocrites? Show me the poll-tax coin!"

And they brought me a denarius. And I said to them,

"Whose head and title is this?"

They answered,

"The emperor's."

Then I said to them,

"Then pay the emperor what belongs to the emperor, and pay God what belongs to God!"

And when they heard it they were amazed, and they went away and left me.

The Resurrection

On the same day some Sadduces came up to me, claiming that there is no resurrection, and they asked me this question:

"Master, Moses said, 'If a man dies without children his

brother shall marry his widow, and raise up a family for him.'
Now there were seven brothers among us. The first of them
married and died, and as he had no children, he left his wife
to his brother; so did the second, and the third, and the rest
of the seven. After them all the woman died. At the resurrection which one's wife will she be? For they all married her."

I said to them,

"The people of this world marry and are married, but those
who are thought worthy to attain that other world and the
resurrection from the dead, neither marry nor are married.
For they cannot die again; they are like the angels, and
through sharing in the resurrection they are sons of God. But
that the dead are raised to life, even Moses indicated in the
passage about the bush, when he calls the Lord 'the God of
Abraham, the God of Isaac, and the God of Jacob.' He is
not the God of dead men but of living, for all men are alive
to him."

When the crowd heard this, they were astounded at my
teaching. Some of the scribes replied,

"Master, that was a fine answer!"

The Greatest Commandment

One of the scribes came up and heard them arguing. He
saw that I had answered them well, and he asked me,

"Which is the first of all the commands?"

I answered,

"The first one is, 'Hear, Israel! The Lord our God is one
lord, and you must love the Lord your God with your whole
heart, your whole soul, your whole mind, and your whole
strength.' And this is the second: 'You must love your
neighbor as you do yourself.' No other command is greater
than these."

The scribe said to me,

"Really, Master, you have finely said that he stands alone,
and there is none but he, and to love him with one's whole

heart, one's whole understanding, and one's whole strength, and to love one's neighbor as one's self is far more than all these burnt-offerings and sacrifices."

And I saw that he answered thoughtfully, and I said to him, "You are not far from the Kingdom of God!"

The Unanswerable Question

While the Pharisees were still gathered there, I asked them, "What do you think about the Christ? Whose son is he?" They said to me,
"David's."
I said to them,
"How is it then that David under the Spirit's influence calls him lord and says,

" 'The Lord has said to my lord, "Sit at my right hand,
Until I put your enemies under your feet" '?

So if David calls him lord, how can he be his son?"
No one could make me any answer, and from that day no one ventured to ask me any more questions.
The mass of the people heard me gladly.

Warnings against the Scribes and Pharisees

Then I said to the crowds and to my disciples,
"The scribes and Pharisees have taken Moses' seat. So do everything they tell you, and observe it all, but do not do as they do, for they talk but do not act. They tie up heavy loads and have them put on men's shoulders, but they will not lift a finger to move them. They do everything they do to have men see it. They wear wide Scripture texts as charms, and they

[143]

wear large tassels, and they like the best places at dinners and the front seats in the synagogues, and to be saluted with respect in public places, and to have men call them 'Rabbi.' But you must not let people call you 'Rabbi,' for you have only one teacher, and you are all brothers. And you must not call anyone on earth your father, for you have only one father, your heavenly Father. And you must not let men call you master, for you have only one master, the Christ. But he who is greatest among you must be your servant. Whoever exalts himself will be humbled and whoever humbles himself will be exalted.

"But alas for you, you hypocritical scribes and Pharisees, for you lock the doors of the Kingdom of Heaven in men's faces, for you will neither go in yourselves nor let those enter who are trying to do so. Alas for you, you hypocritical scribes and Pharisees, for you scour land and sea to make one convert, and when he is converted you make him twice as fit for the pit as you are. Alas for you, you blind guides, who say, 'If anyone swears by the sanctuary, it does not matter, but if anyone swears by the gold of the sanctuary, it is binding.' Blind fools! which is greater, the gold, or the sanctuary that makes the gold sacred? You say, 'If anyone swears by the altar, it does not matter, but if anyone swears by the offering that is on it, it is binding.' You blind men! Which is greater, the offering, or the altar that makes the offering sacred? Anyone who swears by the altar is swearing by it and by everything that is on it, and anyone who swears by the sanctuary is swearing by it and by him who dwells in it; and anyone who swears by heaven is swearing by the throne of God and by him who sits upon it.

"Alas for you, you hypocritical scribes and Pharisees, for you pay tithes on mint, dill, and cummin, and you have let the weightier matters of the Law go—justice, mercy, and integrity. But you should have observed these, without over-looking the others. You blind guides! straining out the gnat, and yet swallowing the camel! Alas for you, you hypocritical scribes and Pharisees, for you clean the outside of the cup and the dish, but inside they are full of greed and self-indulgence. You blind Pharisee! You must first clean the inside of the cup and the dish, so that the outside may be clean too. Alas for you, you hypocritical scribes and Pharisees, for you are like white-washed tombs! They look well on the outside, but inside they are full of the bones of the dead, and all that is unclean. So you outwardly appear to men to be upright, but within you are full of hypocrisy and wickedness.

"Alas for you, you hypocritical scribes and Pharisees, for you build tombs for the prophets, and decorate the monuments of the upright, and say, 'If we had been living in the times of our fathers, we would not have joined them in the murder of the prophets.' So you bear witness against yourselves that you are descended from the murderers of the prophets. Go on and fill up the measure of your forefathers' guilt. You serpents! You brood of snakes! How can you escape being sentenced to the pit? This is why I am going to send you prophets, wise men and scribes, some of whom you will kill and crucify, and some you will flog in your synagogues and hunt from one town to another; it is that on your heads may come all the righteous blood shed on the earth from the blood of Abel the upright to the blood of Zechariah, Barachiah's son, whom you murdered between the sanctuary and the altar! I tell you, all this will come upon this age!

"O Jerusalem, Jerusalem! murdering the prophets, and stoning those who are sent to her, how often I have longed to gather your children around me, as a hen gathers her brood under her wings, but you refused! Now I leave you to yourselves. For I tell you, you will never see me again until you say, 'Blessed be he who comes in the Lord's name!' "

The Widow's Two Mites

And I sat down facing the treasury and watched the people dropping money into it; and many rich people were putting in large sums. A poor widow came up and dropped in two little copper coins which make a cent. I called my disciples to me and said,

"I tell you that this poor widow has put in more than all these others who have been putting money into the treasury. For they all gave of what they had to spare, but she in her want has put in everything she possessed—all she had to live on."

The Gentiles Seek Me

There were some Greeks among those who had come up to worship at the festival, and they went to Philip, who was from Bethsaida in Galilee, and made this request of him:

"Sir, we want to see Jesus."

Philip went and told Andrew, and Andrew and Philip came to me and told me. I answered,

"The time has come for the Son of Man to be glorified. I tell you, unless a grain of wheat falls on the ground and dies, it remains just one grain. But if it dies, it yields a great harvest. Whoever loves his life loses it, and whoever hates his life in this world will preserve it for eternal life. If anyone serves me, he must follow me, and wherever I am found, my servant must be also. If anyone serves me, my Father will show him honor. Now my heart is troubled; what am I to say? Father, save me from this trial! And yet it was for this very purpose that I have come to this trial. Father, honor your own name!"

Then there came a voice from the sky,

"I have honored it, and I will honor it again!"

The crowd of bystanders heard it and said it was thunder. Others said,

"It was an angel speaking to him!"

I answered,

"It was not for my sake that the voice came, but for yours. The judgment of this world is now in progress. Its evil genius is now to be expelled, and if I am lifted up from the ground, I will draw all men to myself."

I said this to show the kind of death I was going to die. The crowd answered,

"We have learned from the Law that the Christ is to remain here forever. So how can you say that the Son of Man must be lifted up? Who is this Son of Man?"

I said to them,

"You will have the light only a little while longer. Go on while you still have the light, so that darkness may not overtake you, for those who go about in the dark do not know where they are going. While you have the light believe in the light, that you may become sons of light."

With these words I went away, and disappeared from them.

The Jews Reject Me

But for all the signs I had shown among them, they refused to believe in me, in fulfilment of the saying of the prophet Isaiah,

"Lord, who has believed our account?
And to whom has the Lord's mighty arm been unveiled?"

So they could not believe; for Isaiah says again,

"He has made their eyes blind and their minds dull,
To keep them from seeing with their eyes, and understanding with their minds,
And turning to me to be cured."

Isaiah said this because he saw my glory; it was of me that he spoke. Yet for all that, even among the leading men, many came to believe in me, but on account of the Pharisees they would not acknowledge it, for fear of being excluded from the synagogues, for they cared more for the approval of men than for the approval of God.

But I cried loudly,

"Whoever believes in me, believes not in me but in him who has sent me; and whoever sees me, sees him who has sent me.

I have come into the world as a light, so that no one who believes in me may have to remain in darkness. If anyone hears my words and disregards them, it is not I that judge him, for I have not come to judge the world but to save the world. Whoever rejects me and refuses to accept my teachings is not without his judge; the very message I have given will be his judge on the Last Day, for I have not spoken on my own account, but the Father who has sent me has himself given me orders what to tell and what to say. And I know his orders mean eternal life. So whatever I say, I say only as the Father has told me."

Discourse Concerning the Future

And I left the Temple and was going away, when my disciples came up to me to call my attention to the Temple buildings. But I answered.

"Do you see all this? I tell you, not one stone will be left here upon another but shall be torn down."

As I was sitting on the Mount of Olives, the disciples came up to me by themselves, and said to me,

"Tell us when this is to happen, and what will be the sign of your coming, and of the close of the age."

I answered.

"Take care that no one misleads you about this. For many will come under my name, and say, 'I am the Christ,' and many will be misled by them. You will hear of wars and rumors of war; do not let yourselves be alarmed. They have to come, but that is not the end. For nation will rise in arms against nation, and kingdom against kingdom, and there will be famines and earthquakes here and there. All this is only the beginning of the sufferings. Then they will hand you over to persecution and they will put you to death, and you will be hated by all the heathen because you bear my name. Then many will fall away and betray one another and hate one another. Many false prophets will appear, and many will be misled by them, and because of the increase of wickedness, most men's love will grow cold. But he who holds out to the end will be saved. But when you see Jerusalem being surrounded by armies, then you must understand that her devastation is at hand. Then those who are in Judea must fly to the hills, those who are in the city must get out of it, and those who are in the country must not go into it, for those are the days of vengeance, when all that is written in the Scriptures will be fulfilled.

"Alas for women who are with child at that time, or who have babies! Pray that it may not be winter when it comes, for there will be such misery in those days as there has never been since the beginning of God's creation until now, and never will be again. If the Lord had not cut those days short, nobody would have escaped, but for the sake of his own chosen people he has cut the days short. If anyone says to you at that time, 'Look! Here is the Christ!' or 'Look! There he is!' do not believe it. For false Christs and false prophets will appear, and they will show signs and wonders to mislead God's chosen people if they can. But you must be on your guard; I have told you all about it beforehand. So if they say to you, 'There he is, in the desert!' do not go out there; 'Here he is, in a room in here!' do not believe it. For just as the lightning starts in the east and flashes to the west, so the coming of the Son of Man will be. Wherever there is a dead body, the vultures will flock.

"But immediately after the misery of those days, the sun will be darkened, and the moon will not shed its light, and the stars will fall from the sky, and the forces of the sky will shake. Then the sign of the Son of Man will appear in the sky, and all the nations of the earth will lament when they see the Son of Man coming on the clouds of the sky, in all his power and splendor. And he will send out his angels with a loud trumpet-call, and they will gather his chosen people from the four winds, from one end of the sky to the other.

"Let the fig tree teach you the lesson. As soon as its branches grow soft and put forth leaves, you know that summer is coming. So when you see all these things, you must know that he is just at the door. I tell you, these things will all happen before the present age passes away. Earth and sky will pass away but my words will never pass away. But about that day or hour no one knows, not even the angels in heaven nor the Son, but only the Father.

"But take care that your hearts are not loaded down with self-indulgence and drunkenness and worldly cares, and that day takes you by surprise, like a trap. For it will come on all who are living anywhere on the face of the earth. But you must be vigilant and always pray that you may succeed in escaping all this that is going to happen, and in standing in the presence of the Son of Man.

"For just as it was in the time of Noah, it will be at the coming of the Son of Man. For just as in those days before the flood people were eating and drinking, marrying and being married, until the very day Noah entered the ark, and knew nothing about it until the flood came and destroyed them all, so it will be at the coming of the Son of Man. Two men will be in the field; one will be taken and one left. Two women will be grinding with the handmill; one will be taken and one left. So you must be on the watch, for you do not know on what day your Master is coming. But you may be sure of this, that if the master of the house had known in what part of the night the thief was coming, he would have been on the watch, and would not have let his house be broken into. Therefore you must be ready too, for the Son of Man is coming at a time when you do not expect him.

"You must look out and be on the alert, for you do not know when it will be time; just as a man when he leaves home to go on a journey, and puts his slaves in charge, each with his duties, gives orders to the watchman to keep watch. So you must be on the watch, for you do not know when the master of the house is coming—in the evening or at midnight or toward daybreak or early in the morning—for fear he should come unexpectedly and find you asleep. And what I am telling you I mean for all—Be on the watch!

"Who then will be the faithful, thoughtful slave whom his master put in charge of his household, to give the members of it their supplies at the proper time? Blessed is that slave if his master when he returns finds him doing it. I tell you, he will put him in charge of all his property. But if he is a bad slave and says to himself, 'My master is going to stay a long time,' and begins to beat the other slaves, and eats and drinks with drunkards, that slave's master will come back some day when he does not expect him, and at some time of which he does not know and will cut him in two, and put him with the hypocrites, to weep and gnash his teeth.

THREE LESSONS TO THE DISCIPLES

The Parable of the Ten Virgins

"Then the Kingdom of Heaven will be like ten bridesmaids who took their lamps and went out to meet the bridegroom. Now five of them were foolish and five were sensible. For the foolish ones brought their lamps but brought no oil with them, but the sensible ones with their lamps brought oil in their flasks. As the bridegroom was slow in coming, they all grew drowsy and fell asleep. But in the middle of the night there was a shout 'Here is the bridegroom! Come out and meet him!' Then all the bridesmaids awoke, and trimmed their lamps. And the foolish ones said to the sensible ones, 'Give us some of your oil, for our lamps are going out.' But the sensible ones answered, 'There may not be enough for us and you. You had better go to the dealers and buy yourselves some.' But while they were gone to buy it, the bridegroom arrived, and the ones that were ready went in with him to the wedding banquet, and the door was closed. Afterward the other bridesmaids came and said, 'Sir! Sir! Open the door for us!' But he answered, 'I tell you, I do not know you!' So you must be on the watch, for you do not know either the day or the hour.

"For it is just like a man who was going on a journey, and called in his slaves, and put his property in their hands. He gave one five thousand dollars, and another two thousand, and another one thousand; to each according to his ability. Then he went away. The man who had received the five thousand dollars immediately went into business with the money, and made five thousand more. In the same way the man who had received the two thousand made two thousand more. But the man who had received the one thousand went away and dug a hole in the ground and hid his masters' money. Long afterward, their master came back and settled accounts with them. And the man who had received the five thousand dollars came up bringing him five thousand more, and said, 'Sir, you put five thousand dollars in my hands; here I have made five thousand more.' His master said to him, 'Well done, my excellent, faithful slave! you have been faithful about a small amount; I will put a large one into your hands. Come, share your master's enjoyment! And the man who had received the two thousand came up and said, 'Sir, you put two thousand dollars into my hands; here I have made two thousand more.' His master said to him, 'Well done, my excellent, faithful slave! you have been faithful about a small amount; I will put a large one into your hands. Come! share your master's enjoyment.' And the man who had received the one thousand came up and said, 'Sir, I knew you were a hard man, who reaped where you had not sown, and gathered where you had not threshed, and I was frightened, and I went and hid your thousand dollars in the ground. Here is your money!" His master answered, 'You wicked, idle slave! You knew that I reaped where I had not sown and gathered where I had not threshed? Then you ought to have put my money in the bank, and then when I came back I would have gotten my property with interest. So take the thousand dollars away from him, and give it to the man who has the ten thousand, for the man who has will have more given him, and will be plentifully supplied, and from the man who has nothing even what he has will be taken away. And put the good-for-nothing slave out into the darkness outside, to weep and grind his teeth there.'

The Judgment Scene

"When the Son of Man comes in his splendor, with all his angels with him, he will take his seat on his glorious throne, and all the nations will be gathered before him, and he will separate them from one another, just as a shepherd separates his sheep from his goats, and he will put the sheep at his right hand and the goats at his left. Then the king will say to those at his right, 'Come, you whom my Father has blessed, take possession of the kingdom which has been destined for you from the creation of the world. For when I was hungry, you gave me food, when I was thirsty you gave me something to drink, when I was a stranger, you invited me to your homes, when I had no clothes, you gave me clothes, when I was sick, you looked after me, when I was in prison, you came to see me.' Then the upright will answer, 'Lord, when did we see you hungry and give you food, or thirsty, and give you something to drink? When did we see you as a stranger, and invite you home, or without clothing, and supply you with it? When did we see you sick or in prison, and go to see you?' The king will answer, 'I tell you, in so far as you did it to one of the humblest of these brothers of mine, you did it to me.' Then he will say to those at his left, 'Begone, you accursed people, to the everlasting fire destined for the devil and his angels! For when I was hungry, you gave me nothing to eat, and when I was thirsty you gave me nothing to drink, when I was a stranger, you did not invite me home, when I had no clothes, you did not supply me, when I was sick and in prison, you did not look after me.' Then they in their turn will answer, 'Lord, when did we see you hungry, or thirsty, or a stranger, or in need of

[153]

clothes, or sick, or in prison, and did not wait upon you?'
Then he will answer, 'I tell you, in so far as you failed to do
it for one of these people who are humblest, you failed to do
it for me.' Then they will go away to everlasting punishment,
and the upright to everlasting life."

The Conspiracy Against Me

When I had finished this discourse I said to my disciples,
"You know that in two days the Passover Festival will come,
and the Son of Man will be handed over to be crucified."

Then the high priests and the elders of the people gathered
in the house of the high priest, whose name was Caiaphas, and
plotted to arrest me by stealth and put me to death. But they
said,

"It must not be during the festival, or there may be a riot."

But Satan entered into Judas, who was called Iscariot, a
member of the Twelve. And he went off and discussed with the
high priests and captains of the Temple how he could betray
me to them, and said,

"What will you give me if I hand him over to you?"

And they counted him out thirty silver pieces. And from that
time he watched for a good opportunity to hand me over to
them without a disturbance.

THURSDAY—THE DAY OF FELLOWSHIP

Preparation for the Passover

On the first day of the festival of Unleavened Bread, on which
it was customary to kill the Passover Lamb, my disciples said
to me,

[154]

"Where do you wish us to go and make the preparations for you to eat the Passover supper?"

So I sent away two of my disciples, saying to them,

"Go into the city, and you will meet a man carrying a pitcher of water. Follow him, and whatever house he goes into, say to the man of the house, 'The Master says, "Where is my room where I can eat the Passover supper with my disciples?" ' And he will show you a large room upstairs, furnished and ready. Make your preparations for us there."

So the disciples started and went into the city, and found everything just as I had told them; and they prepared the Passover supper.

Strife Among the Disciples

When it was evening I came with the Twelve. A dispute also arose among them, as to which one of them ought to be considered the greatest. But I said to them,

"The kings of the heathen lord it over them, and their authorities are given the title of Benefactor. But you are not to do so, but whoever is greatest among you must be like the youngest, and the leader like a servant. For which is greater, the man at the table, or the servant who waits on him? Is not the man at the table? Yet I am like a servant among you. But it is you who have stood by me in my trials. So just as my Father has conferred a kingdom on me, I confer on you the right to eat and drink at my table in my kingdom, and to sit on thrones and judge the twelve tribes of Israel!"

Washing My Disciples' Feet

Before the Passover Festival began, I knew that the time had come for me to leave this world and go to the Father, but I had loved those who were my own in the world, and I loved them to the last. So at supper—the devil having by this time put the thought of betraying me into the mind of Judas Iscariot, Simon's son—I, fully aware that the Father had put everything into his hands, and that I had come from God and was going back to God, rose from the table, took off my outer clothing, and fastened a towel about my waist. Then I poured water into the basin and began to wash the disciples' feet, wiping them with the towel that was about my waist. So I came to Simon Peter. He said to me,

"Master, are you going to wash my feet?"

I answered,

"You cannot understand now what I am doing, but you will learn by and by."

Peter said to me,

"I will never let you wash my feet!"

I answered,

"You will have no share with me unless I wash you."

Simon Peter said to me,

"Master, wash not only my feet but my hands and my face too!"

I said to him,

"Anyone who has bathed only needs to have his feet washed to be altogether clean. And you are already clean—though not all of you." For I knew who was going to betray me, that was why I said, "You are not all of you clean."

When I had washed their feet and put on my clothes and taken my place, I said to them again,

"Do you understand what I have been doing to you? You call me Teacher and Master, and you are right, for that is what I am. If I then, your Master and Teacher, have washed your feet, you ought to wash one another's feet too. For I have set you an example, in order that you may do what I have done to you. I tell you, no slave is superior to his master, and no messenger is greater than the man who sends him. Now that you have this knowledge, you will be blessed if you act upon it. I do not mean all of you; I know whom I have chosen; but let the Scripture be fulfilled:

" 'He who is eating my bread
   Has raised his heel against me.'

From now on I will tell you things before they happen, so that when they do happen you may believe that I am what I say. I assure you, whoever welcomes any messenger of mine welcomes me and whoever welcomes me welcomes him who has sent me."

The Betrayer Pointed Out

After I had said this I was greatly moved and said solemnly,
"I tell you, it is one of you that will betray me!"
The disciples looked at one another in doubt as to which of them I meant. They were deeply hurt and began to say to me one after another,
"Can it be I, Master?"
I answered,
"The man who just dipped his hand in the same dish with me is going to betray me. The Son of Man is to go away as the Scriptures say of him, but alas for the man by whom the Son of Man is betrayed! It would have been better for that man if he had never been born!"
Judas, who betrayed me, said,
"Can it be I, Master?"
I said to him,
"You are right!"
Next to me, at my right at the table, was one of my disciples whom I especially loved. So Simon Peter nodded to him and said to him,
"Tell us whom he means."
He leaned back from where he lay, on my breast, and said to me,
"Master, who is it?"
I answered,
"It is the one to whom I am going to give this piece of bread when I have dipped it in the dish." So I dipped the piece of bread and took it and gave it to Judas, Simon Iscariot's son. After he took the bread, Satan took possession of him. Then I said to him,

"Be quick about your business."

But no one else at the table knew what I meant by telling him this, for some of them thought that as Judas had the purse I meant to say to him, "Buy what we need for the festival," or to have him give something to the poor. So immediately after taking the piece of bread he went out. It was then night.

When he was gone, I said,

"Now the Son of Man has been honored, and God has been honored through him, and God will through himself honor him; he will honor him immediately."

The Lord's Supper

And I said to them,

"I have greatly desired to eat this Passover supper with you before I suffer. For I tell you, I will never eat one again until it reaches its fulfilment in the Kingdom of God."

And I took a loaf of bread and thanked God, and broke it in pieces, and gave it to them, saying,

"Take this and eat it. It is my body!"

And I took the wine-cup and gave thanks and gave it to them, saying,

"You must all drink from it, for this is my blood which ratifies the agreement, and is to be poured out for many people, for the forgiveness of their sins. Take this and share it among you, for I tell you, I will not drink the product of the vine again until the Kingdom of God comes.

The Farewell Conversation

"My children, I am to be with you only a little longer. You will look for me, but, as I said to the Jews, where I am going you cannot follow. I give you a new command: Love one

[158]

another. Just as I have loved you, you must love one another. By this they will all know that you are my disciples—by your love for one another."

Simon Peter said to me,

"Master, where are you going?"

I answered,

"I am going where you cannot follow me now, but you will follow me later."

And I said to them,

"You will all desert me, for the Scriptures say, 'I will strike the shepherd, and the sheep will be scattered.' But after I am raised to life again I will go back to Galilee before you."

But Peter said to me,

"Even if they all desert you, I will not!"

I said to him,

"I tell you, this very night before the cock crows twice you yourself will disown me three times! O Simon, Simon! Satan has obtained permission to sift all of you like wheat, but I have prayed that your own faith may not fail. And afterward you yourself must turn and strengthen your brothers."

But Peter persisted vehemently,

"If I have to die with you, I will never disown you."

And they all said the same thing.

And I said to them,

"When I sent you out without any purse or bag or shoes, was there anything you needed?"

They said,

"No, nothing."

I said to them,

"But now, if a man has a purse let him take it, and a bag too. And a man who has no sword must sell his coat and buy one. For I tell you that this saying of Scripture must find its fulfilment in me: 'He was rated an outlaw.' Yes, that saying about me is to be fulfilled!"

But they said,

"See, Master, here are two swords!"

And I said to them,

"Enough of this!"

"Your minds must not be troubled; you must believe in God,

and believe in me. There are many rooms in my Father's house, if there were not, I would have told you, for I am going away to make ready a place for you. And if I go and make it ready, I will come back and take you with me, so that you may be where I am. You know the way to the place where I am going."

Thomas said to me,

"Master, we do not know where you are going; how can we know the way?"

I said to him,

"I am Way and Truth and Life. No one can come to the Father except through me. If you knew me, you would know my Father also. From now on you do know him and you have seen him."

Philip said to me,

"Master, let us see the Father, and it will satisfy us."

I said to him,

"Have I been with you so long, and yet you, Philip, have not recognized me? Whoever has seen me has seen the Father. How can you say, 'Let us see the Father'? Do you not believe that I am in union with the Father and the Father is in union with me? I am not the source of the words that I say to you, but the Father who is united with me is doing these things himself. You must believe that I am in union with the Father and that the Father is in union with me, or else you must believe because of the things themselves. I tell you, whoever believes in me will do such things as I do, and things greater yet, because I am going to the Father. Anything you ask for as followers of mine I will grant, so that the Father may be honored through the Son. I will grant anything you ask me for as my followers.

"If you really love me, you will observe my commands. And I will ask the Father and he will give you another Helper to be with you always. It is the Spirit of Truth. The world cannot obtain that Spirit, because it does not see it or recognize it; you recognize it because it stays with you and is within you. I am not going to leave you friendless. I am coming back to you. In a little while the world will not see me any more, but you will still see me, because I shall live on, and you will live on too. When that day comes you will know that I am in union with my Father and you are with me and I am with you. It is he who has my commands and observes them that really loves me, and whoever loves me will be loved by my Father, and I will love him and show myself to him."

Judas (not Judas Iscariot), said to me,

"Master, how does it happen that you are going to show yourself to us and not to the world?"

I answered,

"Anyone who loves me will observe my teaching, and my Father will love him and we will come to him and live with him. No one who does not love me will observe my teaching, and yet the teaching you are listening to is not mine but is that of him who has sent me.

"I have told you this while I am still staying with you, but the Helper, the holy Spirit which the Father will send in my place, will teach you everything and remind you of everything that I have told you. I leave you a blessing; my peace I give unto you. I do not give it to you as the world gives. Your minds must not be troubled or afraid. You have heard me say that I am going away and am coming back to you; if you loved me you would be glad that I am going to the Father, for the Father is greater than I. And I have told you of it now before it happens, in order that when it happens you may believe in me. I shall not talk much more with you, for the evil genius of the world is coming. He has nothing in common with me, but he is coming that the world may know that I love the Father and am doing what he has commanded me to do.

"I am the true vine, and my Father is the cultivator. Any branch of mine that does not bear fruit he trims away, and he prunes every branch that bears fruit, to make it bear more. You are pruned already because of the teaching that I have given you. You must remain united to me and I will remain united to you. Just as no branch can bear fruit by itself unless it remains united to the vine, you cannot unless you remain united to me. I am the vine, you are the branches. Anyone who remains united to me, with me united to him, will be very fruitful, for you cannot do anything apart from me. Anyone who does not remain united to me is thrown away like a branch and withers up, and they gather them and throw them into the fire and burn them. If you remain united to me and my words remain in your hearts, ask for whatever you please and you shall have it. When you are very fruitful and show yourselves to be disciples of mine, my Father is honored. I have loved you just as the Father has loved me. You must retain my love. If you keep my commands you will retain my love, just as I have observed the Father's commands and retain his love. I have told you all this so that you may have the happiness that I have had, and your happiness may be complete. The command that I give you is to love one another just as I have loved you. No one can show greater love than by giving up his life for his friends. You are my friends if you do what I command you to do. I do not call you slaves any longer, for a slave does not know what his master is doing, but now I call you friends, for I have made known to you everything that I have learned from my Father. It was not you who chose me, it is I that have chosen you, and appointed you to go and bear fruit—fruit that shall be lasting, so that the Father may grant you whatever you ask him for as my followers.

"What I command you to do is to love one another. If the world hates you, remember that it hated me first. If you belonged to the world, the world would love what was its own. But it is because you do not belong to the world, but I have selected you from the world, that the world hates you. Remember what I said to you: No slave is greater than his master. If they have persecuted me they will persecute you too. If they have observed my teaching, they will observe yours too. But they will do all this to you on my account because they do not understand him who sent me. If I had not come and spoken to them, they would not have been guilty of sin, but as it is, they have no excuse for their sin. Whoever hates me hates my Father also. If I had not done things before them that no one else ever did they would not be guilty of sin. But as it is, they have seen both me and my Father, and they have hated us both. But the saying of their Law, 'They hated me without cause,' must be fulfilled. When the Helper comes whom I will send to you from the Father—that Spirit of Truth that comes from the Father—he will bear testimony to me, and you must bear testimony too, because you have been with me from the first.

"I have told you this to keep you from faltering. They will exclude you from their synagogues; why, the time is coming when anyone who kills you will think he is doing religious service to God. They will do this because they do not know the Father or me. But I have told you about these things in order that when the time comes for them to happen, you may remember that I told you of them. I did not tell you this at first because I was still staying with you. But now I am going away to him who sent me, and not one of you asks me where I am going, but your minds are full of sorrow because I have told you this. Yet it is only the truth when I tell you that it is better for you that I should go away. For if I do not go, the Helper will not come to you, but if I go I will send him to you. When he comes, he will bring conviction to the world about sin and uprightness and judgment; about sin, as shown in their not believing in me; about uprightness, as shown by my going away to the Father, where you can no longer see me; and about judgment, as shown by the condemnation of the evil genius of this world. I have much more to tell you, but you cannot take it in now, but when the Spirit of Truth comes, he will guide you into the full truth, for he will not speak for himself but will tell what he hears, and will announce to you the things that are to come. He will do honor to me, for he will take what is mine and communicate it to you. All that the Father has belongs to me. That is why I said that he will take what is mine and communicate it to you. . . .

"In a little while you will not see me any longer, and a little while after, you will see me again."

Then some of my disciples said to one another,

"What does he mean when he tells us, 'In a little while you will not see me any longer, and a little while after, you will see me again,' and 'Because I am going away to the Father'?" So they kept saying "What does he mean by 'In a little while'? We do not know what he is talking about."

I saw that they wanted to ask me a question, and I said to them,

"Are you asking one another about my saying 'In a little while you will not see me any longer, and a little while after, you will see me again'? I tell you, you will weep and wail while the world will be happy; you will grieve, but your grief will change to happiness. When a woman is in labor she is sorrowful, for her time has come; but when the child is born, she forgets her pain in her joy that a human being has been brought into the world. So you, too, are sorrowful now; but I will see you again, and your hearts will be happy, and no one will rob you of your happiness. When that time comes, you will not ask me any questions; I tell you, whatever you ask the Father for, he will give you as my followers. Hitherto you have not asked for anything as my followers, but now ask, and you will receive, so that your happiness may be complete.

"I have said all this to you in figurative language, but a time is coming when I shall not do so any longer, but will tell you plainly about the Father. When that time comes you will ask as my followers, and I do not promise to intercede with the Father for you, for the Father loves you himself because you love me and believe that I have come from the Father. I did come from the Father and enter the world. Now I am leaving the world again and going back to the Father."

My disciples said,

"Why, now you are talking plainly and not speaking figuratively at all. Now we know that you know everything and do not need to have anyone ask you questions. This makes us believe that you have really come from God."

I answered,

"Do you believe that now? Why, a time is coming—it has already come!—when you will all be scattered to your homes and will leave me alone. And yet I am not alone, for the Father is with me. I have told you all this, so that through me you may find peace. In the world you have trouble; but take courage! I have conquered the world."

The Intercessory Prayer

When I had said all this I raised my eyes to heaven and said, "Father, the time has come. Do honor to your son, that your son may do honor to you, just as you have done in giving him power over all mankind, so that he may give eternal life to all whom you have given him. And eternal life means knowing you as the only true God, and knowing Jesus your messenger as Christ. I have done honor to you here on earth, by completing the work which you gave me to do. Now, Father, do such honor to me in your presence as I had done me there before the world existed.

"I have revealed your real self to the men you gave me from the world. They were yours and you gave them to me, and they have obeyed your message. Now at last they know that all that you have given me comes from you, for I have given them the truths that you gave me, and they have accepted them and been convinced that I came from you, and they believe that you sent me. I have a request to make for them. I make no request for the world, but only for those whom you have given me, for they are yours—all that is mine is yours and what is yours is mine—and they have done me honor. Now I am to be no longer in this world, but they are to remain in the world, while I return to you. Holy Father, keep them by your power which you gave me, so that they may be one just as we are. As long as I was with them I kept them by your power which you gave me, and I protected them, and not one of them was lost (except the one who was destined to be lost), so that what the Scripture says might come true. But now I am coming to you, and I say this here in this world in order that they may have the happiness that I feel fully realized in their own hearts. I have given them your message, and the world has come to hate them, for they do not belong to the world any more than I belong to the world. I do not ask you to take them away from the world, but to keep them from evil. They do not belong to the world any more than I belong to the world. Consecrate them by truth. Your message is truth. Just as you sent me to the world, I have sent them to the world. And it is for their sake that I consecrate myself, that they also may be consecrated by truth.

"It is not for them only that I make this request. It is also for those who through their message come to believe in me. Let them all be one. Just as you, Father, are in union with me and I am with you, let them be in union with us, so that the world may believe that you sent me. I have given them the glory that you gave me, so that they may be one just as we are, I in union with them and you with me, so that they may be perfectly unified, and the world may recognize that you sent me and that you love them just as you loved me. Father, I wish to have those whom you have given me, for you loved me before the creation of the world. Righteous Father, though the world did not know you, I knew you, and these men knew that you had sent me. I have made your self known to them and I will do so still, so that the love which you have had for me may be in their hearts, and I may be there also."

When we had sung a hymn, we went out into the mount of Olives.*

FRIDAY—THE DAY OF SUFFERING

The Agony of Gethsemane

We came to a place called Gethsemane, and I said to my disciples,

"Sit down here while I pray."

And I took Peter, James, and John along with me, and I began to feel distress and dread, and I said to them,

* This sentence from The Authorized Version.

"My heart is almost breaking. You must stay here and keep watch." And I went on a little way and threw myself on the ground and prayed that if it were possible I might be spared the hour of trial; and I said,

"Abba!" that is, Father, "anything is possible for you! Take this cup away from me! Yet not what I please but what you do!"

When I got up from my prayer, I went to the disciples and found them asleep from sorrow. And I said to Peter,

"Then were you not able to watch with me for one hour? You must all watch, and pray that you may not be exposed to trial! One's spirit is eager, but flesh and blood are weak!"

I went away again a second time and prayed, saying,

"My Father, if it cannot pass by me without my drinking it, your will be done!"

When I came back I found them asleep again, for they could hardly keep their eyes open. And I left them and went away again and prayed a third time, in the same words as before. Then I came back to the disciples and said to them,

"Are you still sleeping and taking your rest? See, the time has come for the Son of Man to be handed over to wicked men! Get up! Let us be going! Look! Here comes my betrayer!"

The Betrayal and Arrest

Just at that moment, while I was still speaking, Judas, who was one of the Twelve, came up, and with him a crowd of men with swords and clubs, from the high priests, scribes, and elders. Now the man who betrayed me had given them a signal, saying,

"The one I kiss is the man. Seize him and take him safely away."

So when he came he went straight up to me and said, "Master!" and kissed me affectionately. I said to him,

"Would you betray the Son of Man with a kiss?"

Then I, as I knew everything that was going to happen to me, came forward and said to them,

"Who is it you are looking for?"

They answered,

"Jesus of Nazareth."

I said to them,

"I am he."

Judas who betrayed me was standing among them. When I said to them, "I am he," they drew back and fell to the ground. Then I asked them again,

"Who is it you are looking for?"

"Jesus of Nazareth."

I answered,

"I have told you that I am he, so if you are looking for me, let these men go." This was to fulfil the saying I had uttered, "I have not lost one of those whom you have given me."

Those who were about me saw what was coming and said,

"Master, shall we use our swords?"

Then Simon Peter, who had a sword with him, drew it and struck at the high priest's slave and cut off his right ear. The slave's name was Malchus. But I answered,

"Let me do this much!"

And I touched his ear and healed him. Then I said to Peter,

"Put your sword back where it belongs! For all who draw the sword will die by the sword. Do you suppose I cannot appeal to my Father, and he would at once furnish me more than twelve legions of angels? But then how are the Scriptures to be fulfilled, which say that this must happen? Shall I not drink the cup which the Father has offered me?"

I spoke and said to them,

"Have you come out to arrest me with swords and clubs, as though I were a robber? I have been among you day after day in the Temple teaching, and you never seized me. But let the Scriptures be fulfilled?"

Then all the disciples left and made their escape.

And a young man followed me with nothing but a linen cloth

about his body; and they seized him, but he left the cloth behind and ran away naked.

The Trial before the Jewish Authorities

So the garrison and the colonel and the attendants of the Jews seized me and bound me, and they took me first to Annas. For he was the father-in-law of Caiaphas, who was high priest that year. Now it was Caiaphas who had advised the Jews that it was for their interest that one man should die for the people.

But Simon Peter and another disciple followed me. This other disciple was an acquaintance of the high priest, and he went on with me into the high priest's courtyard, while Peter stood outside at the door. So this other disciple, the acquaintance of the high priest, went out and spoke to the woman at the door and brought Peter in. The maid at the door said to Peter,

"Are you also one of this man's disciples?"

He said,

"No, I am not."

As it was cold the slaves and attendants had made a charcoal fire, and stood about it warming themselves. And Peter also was among them, standing and warming himself.

Then the high priest questioned me about my disciples and my teaching. I answered,

"I have spoken openly to the world. I have always taught in synagogues or in the Temple where all the Jews meet together, and I have said nothing in secret. Why do you question me? Ask those who have heard me what it was that I said to them. They will know what I have said."

When I said this, one of the attendants who stood near struck me and said,

"Is that the way you answer the high priest?"

I replied,

"If I have said anything wrong, testify to it; but if what I have said is true, why do you strike me?"

So Annas sent me over still bound to Caiaphas the high priest.

The high priests and the whole council tried to get evidence against me in order to put me to death, and they could find none, for while many gave false testimony against me their evidence did not agree. Some got up and gave false testimony against me to this effect:

"We ourselves have heard him say, 'I will tear down this sanctuary built by men's hands, and in three days I will build another, made without hands.' "

And even then their evidence did not agree. Then the high priest got up and came forward into the center and asked me,

"Have you no answer to make? What about their evidence against you?"

But I was silent and made no answer. And the high priest said to me,

"I charge you, on your oath, by the living God, tell us whether you are the Christ, the son of God."

I said to him,

"It is true. But I tell you you will soon see the Son of Man seated at the right hand of the Almighty and coming upon the clouds of the sky!"

Then the high priest tore his clothing and said,

"He has uttered blasphemy! What do we want of witnesses now? Here you have heard his blasphemy! What is your decision?"

They answered,

"He deserves death."

Then they spat in my face and struck me, and others slapped me, saying,

"Show us you are a prophet, you Christ! Who was it that struck you?"

The Denial of Peter

While Peter was down in the courtyard, one of the high priest's maids came up, and seeing Peter warming himself, she looked at him and said,

"You were with this Jesus of Nazareth too!"

But he denied it, saying,

"I do not know or understand what you mean."

A little while after the bystanders came up to Peter and said,

"You are certainly one of them too, for your accent shows it!"

Then he started to swear with the strongest oaths,

"I do not know the man!"

And at that moment a cock crowed. And Peter remembered my words when I had said,

"Before a cock crows, you will disown me three times!"

And he went outside and wept bitterly.

The Remorse of Judas

Then Judas who had betrayed me, when he saw that I had been condemned, in his remorse brought back the thirty silver pieces to the high priests and elders, and said,

"I did wrong when I handed an innocent man over to death!"

They said,

"What is that to us? You see to it yourself."

And he threw down the silver and left the Temple and went off and hung himself. The high priests gathered up the money, and they said,

"It is not legal to put this into the Temple treasury, for it is blood money."

So after consultation they bought with it the Potter's Field as a burial ground for strangers. For this reason that piece of ground has ever since been called the Field of Blood. So the words spoken by the prophet Jeremiah were fulfilled: "They took the thirty silver pieces, the price of the one whose price had been fixed, on whom some of the Israelites had set a price, and gave them for the Potter's Field as the Lord directed me."

The Trial Before Pilate

Then they took me from Caiaphas to the governor's house. It was early in the morning, and they would not go into the governor's house themselves, to avoid being ceremonially defiled and to be able to eat the Passover supper. So Pilate came outside to them and said,

"What charge do you make against this man?"

They answered,

"If he were not a criminal, we would not have turned him over to you."

Pilate said to them,

"Take him yourselves, and try him by your law."

The Jews said to him,

"We have no authority to put anyone to death."

This was to fulfil what I said when I declared how I was to die.

And they made this charge against me:

"Here is a man whom we have found misleading our nation, and forbidding the payment of taxes to the emperor, and claiming to be an anointed king himself."

And while the high priests and elders were making their charges against me, I made no answer. Then Pilate said to me,

"Do you not hear what evidence they are bringing against you?"

And I made him no reply to even a single accusation, so that the governor was greatly surprised.

So Pilate went back into the governor's house and called me and said to me,

"Are you the king of the Jews?"

I answered,

"Did you think of that yourself, or has someone else said it to you about me?"

Pilate answered,

"Do you take me for a Jew? Your own people and the high priests handed you over to me. What offense have you committed?"

I answered,

"My kingdom is not a kingdom of this world. If my kingdom were a kingdom of this world, my men would have fought to keep me from being handed over to the Jews. But as it is, my kingdom has no such origin."

Pilate said to me,

"Then you are a king?"

I answered,

"As you say, I am a king. It was for this that I was born and for this that I came to the world, to give testimony for truth. Everyone who is on the side of truth listens to my voice."

Pilate said to me,

"What is truth!"

With these words he went outside again to the Jews, and said to them,

"I cannot find anything criminal about this man."

But they persisted and said,

"He is stirring up the people all over Judea by his teaching. He began in Galilee and he has come here."

When Pilate heard this, he asked if I were a Galilean and learning that I belonged to Herod's jurisdiction, he turned me over to Herod, for Herod was in Jerusalem at that time.

Before Herod

When Herod saw me he was delighted, for he had wanted for a long time to see me, because he had heard about me and he hoped to see some wonder done by me. And he questioned me at some length, but I made him no answer. Meanwhile the high priests and the scribes stood by and vehemently accused me. And Herod and his guards made light of me and ridiculed me, and they put a gorgeous robe on me and sent me back to Pilate. And Herod and Pilate became friends that day, for they had been at enmity before.

The Trial Before Pilate Resumed

Pilate summoned the high priests and the leading members of the council and the people, and said to them,

"You brought this man before me charged with misleading the people, and here I have examined him before you and not found him guilty of any of the things that you accuse him of. Neither has Herod, for he has sent him back to us. You see he has done nothing to call for his death. So I will teach him a lesson and let him go."

Now at festival time the governor was accustomed to release for the people any prisoner whom they chose, and at this time there was a notorious prisoner named Barabbas, among some revolutionaries who in their outbreak had committed murder. And a crowd of people came up and started to ask him for the usual favor. Pilate asked them,

"Do you want me to set the king of the Jews free for you?"

For he knew that the high priests had handed me over to him out of envy. But the high priests stirred up the crowd to get him to set Barabbas free for them instead. And Pilate again said to them,

"Then what shall I do with the man you call the king of the Jews?"

They shouted back,

"Crucify him!"

And he said to them a third time,

"Why, what has he done that is wrong? For I have found nothing about him to call for his death. So I will teach him a lesson and let him go."

Then Pilate took me and had me flogged.

Then the soldiers took me inside the courtyard, that is, of the governor's residence, and they called the whole battalion together. And they stripped me and put a red cloak on me, and made a wreath of thorns and put it on my head, and they put a stick in my hand, and knelt down before me in mockery, saying,

"Long live the king of the Jews!"

And they spat at me, and took the stick and struck me on the head.

And Pilate went outside again and said to the Jews,

"See! I will bring him out to you, to show you that I can find nothing to charge him with."

So I came out, still wearing the wreath of thorns and the purple coat. And Pilate said to them,

"Here is the man!"

When the high priests and their attendants saw me, they shouted,

"Have him crucified! Have him crucified!"

Pilate said to them,

"Take him yourselves and have him crucified, for I can find nothing to charge him with."

The Jews answered,

"We have a law, and by our law he deserves death, for declaring himself to be a son of God."

When Pilate heard that, he was more frightened than before and he went back into the governor's house and said to me,

"Where do you come from?"

But I made no answer. Then Pilate said to me,

"Do you refuse to speak to me? Do you not know that it is in my power to release you or to have you crucified?"

I answered him,

"You would have no power at all over me, if it were not given to you from above. So you are less guilty than the man who betrayed me to you."

This made Pilate try to find a way to let me go, but the Jews shouted,

"If you let him go, you are no friend of the emperor's! Anyone who calls himself a king utters treason against the emperor!"

When Pilate heard that, he had me brought out and had me sit in the judge's seat in the place they call the Stone Platform, or in Hebrew, Gabbatha. It was the day of Preparation for the Passover, and it was about noon. And Pilate said to the Jews,

"There is your king!"

At that they shouted,

"Kill him! Kill him! Have him crucified!"

Pilate said to them,

"Am I to crucify your king?"

The high priests answered,

"We have no king but the emperor!"

When Pilate saw that he was gaining nothing but that riot was beginning instead, he took some water and washed his hands in the presence of the crowd, saying,

"I am not responsible for this man's death; you must see to it yourselves."

And all the people answered,

"His blood be on us and on our children!"

They persisted with loud outcries in demanding that I be crucified, and their shouting won. And Pilate pronounced sentence that what they asked for should be done. He released the man they asked for, who had been put in prison for riot and murder, and handed me over to their will.

And when they had finished making sport of me, they took

off the cloak, and put my own clothes on me, and led me away to be crucified.

The Sorrowful Way

So they took me, and I went out carrying the cross by myself. They seized a man named Simon, from Cyrene, the father of Alexander and Rufus, who was coming in from the country, and put the cross on his back, for him to carry behind me. We were followed by a great crowd of people and of women who were beating their breasts and lamenting me. But I turned to them and said,

"Women of Jerusalem, do not weep for me but weep for yourselves and for your children, for a time is coming when they will say, 'Happy are the childless women, and those who have never borne or nursed children!' Then people will begin to say to the mountains, 'Fall on us!' and to the hills, 'Cover us up!' For if this is what they do when the wood is green, what will happen when it is dry?"

Two criminals were also led out to execution with me.

The Crucifixion

When we came to a place called Golgotha, which means the Place of the Skull, they offered me a drink of wine mixed with gall, and when I tasted it I would not drink it.

There they crucified me, with two robbers, one on each side and I in the middle.

Pilate had written a placard and had it put on the cross; it read "Jesus the Nazarene, the king of the Jews." Many of the Jews read this placard, for the place where I was crucified was near the city, and it was written in Hebrew, Latin, and Greek. So the Jewish high priests said to Pilate,

"Do not write 'The king of the Jews,' but write 'He said, I am the king of the Jews.' "

Pilate answered,

"What I have written, I have written!"

When the soldiers had crucified me, they took my clothes and divided them into four parts, one for each soldier, besides my shirt. Now my shirt had no seam; it was woven in one piece from top to bottom.

So they said to one another, "Let us not tear it, but let us draw lots for it to see who gets it."

This was to fulfil what the Scripture says, "They divided my garments among them, and for my clothing they cast lots."

And the passers-by jeered at me, shaking their heads and saying,

"You who would tear down the sanctuary, and build one in three days, save yourself! If you are the Son of God, come down from the cross!"

And the high priests, too, made sport of me with the scribes and elders, and said,

"He saved others, but he cannot save himself! He is King of Israel; let him come down from the cross now, and we will believe in him. He trusts in God; let God deliver him if he cares for him, for he said he was God's son."

One of the criminals who were hanging there, abused me, saying,

"Are you not the Christ? Save yourself and us too!"

But the other reproved him and said,

"Have you no fear even of God when you are suffering the same penalty? And we are suffering it justly, for we are only getting our deserts, but this man has done nothing wrong."

And he said,

"Jesus, remember me when you come into your kingdom!"

And I said to him,

"I tell you, you will be in Paradise with me today!"

Near my cross stood my mother and her sister Mary, the daughter of Clopas, and Mary of Magdala. Seeing my mother and the disciple whom I loved standing near, I said to my mother,

"This is your son!"

[178]

Then I said to my disciple,

"There is your mother." And from that time my disciple took her into his own home.

Now from noon there was darkness over the whole country until three o'clock. And about three, I called out loudly,

"Eloi, Eloi, lama sabachthani?" that is, "My God! My God! Why have you forsaken me?"

Some of the bystanders when they heard it said,

"The man is calling for Elijah!"

After that, I, knowing that everything was now finished, to fulfil the saying of Scripture, said,

"I am thirsty."

A bowl of sour wine was standing there. So they put a sponge soaked in the wine on a pike and held it to my lips. When I had taken the wine, I said,

"It is finished!"

Then I gave a loud cry, and said,

"Father, I intrust my spirit to your hands!"

With these words I expired.

And at once the curtain of the sanctuary was torn in two from top to bottom. The earth shook, the rocks split, the tombs opened, and many of the saints who had fallen asleep rose and left their tombs and after my resurrection went into the holy city and showed themselves to many people. And the captain and the men with him who were watching me, when they saw the earthquake and all that was happening, were dreadfully frightened and said,

"He surely must have been a son of God!"

And all the crowds that had collected for the sight, when they saw what happened, returned to the city beating their breasts. There were several women there watching from a distance who had followed me from Galilee to wait upon me, among them Mary of Magdala, Mary the mother of James and Joseph, and the mother of Zebedee's sons.

As it was the day of Preparation for the Passover, in order that the bodies might not be left on the crosses over the Sabbath, for that Sabbath was an especially important one, the Jews asked Pilate to have the men's legs broken and the bodies removed. So the soldiers went and broke the legs of the first

man and then of the other who had been crucified with me. But when they came to me they saw that I was dead already, and they did not break my legs, but one of the soldiers thrust a lance into my side, and blood and water immediately flowed out. This happened to fulfil what the Scripture says:
"Not one of its bones will be broken."
Moreover, it says in another place,
"They shall look at the man whom they pierced."

The Burial

In the evening a rich man named Joseph, from Arimathea, a highly respected member of the council, came. He went to Pilate and asked him for my body. Pilate wondered whether I was dead already, and he sent for the captain and asked whether I was dead yet, and when he learned from the captain that I was, he gave Joseph permission to take my body. So Joseph came and took my body down. And Nicodemus also, who had first come to me at night, came, taking a roll of myrrh and aloes weighing about a hundred pounds. So they took my body, and wrapped it with the spices in bandages, in the Jewish way of preparing bodies for burial. There was a garden at the place where I had been crucified, and in the garden was a new tomb in which no one had yet been laid. So because it was the Jewish Preparation day, and the tomb hewn out of the rock was close by, they put me there, and rolled a stone against the doorway of the tomb. And Mary of Magdala and Mary, Joses' mother, were looking on and saw where I was put. Then they went home, and prepared spices and perfumes.

On the next day, that is, the day after the Preparation Day, the high priests and Pharisees went in a body to Pilate and said:

"Sir, we remember that when this impostor was alive he said, 'After three days I will rise again.' Give orders therefore, to have the tomb closely guarded till the third day, so that his disciples cannot come and steal him, and then tell the people that he is risen from the dead, and that delusion be worse than the other was."

Pilate said to them,

"Take a guard of soldiers, and go and make it as secure as you can."

So they went and set a guard and put a seal on the stone.

THE RESURRECTION

Sunday—The Day of Resurrection

The Earthquake

There was a great earthquake. For an angel of the Lord came down from heaven and went and rolled the stone back and sat upon it. His appearance was like lightning and his clothing was as white as snow. The men on guard trembled with fear of him, and became like dead men.

The Appearance to the Women

When the Sabbath was over, Mary of Magdala, Mary, James' mother, and Salome bought spices, in order to come and anoint me. Then very early on the first day of the week they came to the tomb, when the sun had just risen. And they said to one another,

"Who will roll the stone back from the doorway of the tomb for us?"

And they looked up and saw that the stone had been rolled

back, for it was very large. And when they went into the tomb they saw a young man in a white robe sitting at the right, and they were utterly amazed. But he said to them,

"You must not be amazed. You are looking for Jesus of Nazareth who was crucified. He has risen, he is not here. See! This is where they laid him. But go and say to his disciples and to Peter, 'He is going before you to Galilee; you will see him there, just as he told you.'"

And they hurried away from the tomb frightened and yet overjoyed, and ran to tell the news to my disciples.

Report of the Watch

While they were on their way, some of the guard went into the city and reported to the high priests all that had happened. And they got together and consulted with the elders, and gave the soldiers a large sum of money, and said to them,

"Tell people that his disciples came in the night and stole him away while you were asleep. And if news of it reaches the governor, we will satisfy him, and see that you do not get into trouble."

So they took the money and did as they were told. And this story has been current among the Jews ever since.

Mary of Magdala went to Simon Peter and the other disciple who was dear to me, and said to them,

"They have taken the Master out of the tomb, and we do not know where they have put him."

So Peter and the other disciple went out of the city and started for the tomb. And they both ran, and the other disciple ran faster than Peter and got to the tomb first. And he stooped down and saw the bandages lying on the ground, but he did not go in. Then Simon Peter came up behind him, and he went inside the tomb, and saw the bandages lying on the ground, and the handkerchief that had been over my face was not on the ground with the bandages, but folded up by itself. Then the other disciple who had reached the tomb first went inside too, and saw and was convinced. For they did not yet understand the statement of Scripture that I must rise from the dead. So the disciples went home again.

The Appearance to Mary

But Mary stood just outside the tomb, weeping. And as she wept she looked down into the tomb, and saw two angels in white sitting where my body had been, one at the head and one at the feet. And they said to her,

"Why are you weeping?"

She said to them,

"They have taken my Master away, and I do not know where they have put him."

As she said this she turned around and saw me standing there, but she did not know that it was I. I said to her,

"Why are you weeping? Whom are you looking for?"

She, supposing that I was the gardener, said to me,

"If it was you, sir, that carried him away, tell me where you have put him, and I will take him away."

"Mary!" I said,

She turned and said to me in Hebrew,

"Rabboni!" which means Master.

I said to her,

"You must not cling to me, for I have not yet gone up to my Father, but go to my brothers and say to them that I am going up to my Father and your Father, to my God and your God."

Mary of Magdala went and declared to the disciples,

"I have seen the Master!"

and she told them that I had said this to her.

The Appearance at Emmaus

That same day two of them were going to a village called Emmaus, about seven miles from Jerusalem, and they were talking together about all these things that had happened. And as they were talking and discussing them, I myself came up and went with them, but they were prevented from recognizing me. And I said to them,

"What is all this that you are discussing with each other on your way?"

They stopped sadly, and one of them named Cleopas said to me,

"Are you the only visitor to Jerusalem who does not know what has happened there lately?"

And I said,

"What is it?"

They said to me,

"About Jesus of Nazareth, who in the eyes of God and of all the people was a prophet mighty in deed and word, and how the high priests and our leading men gave him up to be sentenced to death, and had him crucified. But we were hoping that he was to be the deliverer of Israel. Why, besides all this, it is three days since it happened. But some women of our number have astounded us. They went to the tomb early this morning and could not find his body, but came back and said that they had actually seen a vision of angels who said that he was alive. Then some of our party went to the tomb and found things just as the women had said, but they did not see him."

Then I said to them,

"How foolish you are and how slow to believe all that the prophets have said! Did not the Christ have to suffer thus before entering upon his glory?"

And I began with Moses and all the prophets and explained

[184]

to them the passages all through the Scriptures that referred to myself. When we reached the village to which they were going, I acted as though I were going on, but they urged me not to, and said,

"Stay with us, for it is getting toward evening, and the day is nearly over."

So I went in to stay with them. And when I took my place with them at table, I took the bread and blessed it and broke it in pieces and handed it to them. Then their eyes were opened and they knew me, and I vanished from them. And they said to each other,

"Did not our hearts glow when he was talking to us on the road, and was explaining the Scriptures to us?"

And they got up immediately and went back to Jerusalem, and found the eleven and their party all together, and learned from them that I had really risen and had been seen by Simon. And they told what had happened on the road, and how they had known me when I broke the bread in pieces.

The Appearance to the Disciples

When it was evening on that first day after the Sabbath, and the doors of the house where the disciples met were locked for fear of the Jews, I came in and stood among them and said to them,

"Peace be with you!"

They were startled and panic stricken, and thought they saw a ghost. But I said to them,

"Why are you so disturbed, and why do doubts arise in your minds? Look at my hands and feet, for it is I myself! Feel of me and see, for a ghost has not flesh and bones, as you see I have."

When I said this I showed them my hands and my feet.

But they could not yet believe it for sheer joy and they were amazed. And I said to them,

"Have you anything here to eat?"

And they gave me a piece of broiled fish, and I took it and ate it before their eyes.

Then I said to them again,

"Peace be with you! Just as my Father sent me forth so I now send you."

As I said this I breathed upon them, and said,

"Receive the holy Spirit! If you forgive any men's sins, they are forgiven them, and if you fix any men's sins upon them, they will remain fixed."

EIGHT DAYS AFTER THE RESURRECTION DAY

The Appearance to Thomas

But Thomas, one of the Twelve, who was called the Twin, was not with them when I came in. So the rest of the disciples said to him.

"We have seen the Master!"

But he said to them,

"Unless I see the marks of the nails in his hands, and put my finger into them, and put my hand into his side, I will never believe it!"

Eight days later, the disciples were again in the house, and Thomas was with them. Although the doors were locked, I came in and stood among them, and said,

"Peace be with you!"

Then I said to Thomas,

"Put your finger here and look at my hands, and take your hand and put it in my side, and be no longer unbelieving, but believe!"

Thomas answered me,

"My Master and my God!"

I said to him,

"Is it because you have seen me that you believe? Blessed be those who believe without having seen me!"

I reproached them for their obstinacy and want of faith because they had not believed those who had seen me after I had been raised from the dead. And I said unto them,

"Go to all the world and preach the good news to all the world. He who believes it and is baptized will be saved, but he who does not believe it will be condemned. And signs like these will attend those who believe; with my name they will drive out demons; they will speak in foreign tongues; they will take snakes into their hands, and if they drink poison it will not hurt them; they will lay their hands on the sick and they will get well."

The Appearance to the Seven by the Sea

After this I again showed myself to the disciples at the Sea of Tiberias, and I did so in this way. Simon Peter, Thomas called the Twin, Nathanael, of Cana in Galilee, the sons of Zebedee, and two other disciples of mine were all together. Simon Peter said to them,

"I am going fishing."

They said to him,

"We will go with you."

They went out and got into the boat, and that night they caught nothing. But just as day was breaking, I stood on the beach, though the disciples did not know that it was I. So I said to them,

"Children, have you any fish?"

They answered,

"No."

"Throw your net in on the right of the boat," I said to them, "and you will find them."

They did so, and they could not haul it in for the quantity of fish in it. Then the disciple who was dear to me said to Peter,

"It is the Master!"

When Simon Peter heard that it was I, he put on his clothes, for he had taken them off, and sprang into the sea. The rest of the disciples followed in the boat, for they were not far from land, only about a hundred yards, dragging in the net full of fish. When they landed they saw a charcoal fire burning, with a fish on it, and some bread. I said to them,

"Bring some of the fish you have just caught."

So Simon Peter got into the boat, and hauled the net ashore, full of large fish, a hundred and fifty-three of them, and though there were so many, the net was not torn. I said to them,

"Come and have breakfast."

None of the disciples dared to ask me who I was, for they knew it was I. I went and got the bread and gave it to them, and the fish also. This was the third time that I showed myself to my disciples, after I had risen from the dead.

When they had finished breakfast, I said to Simon Peter,

"Simon, son of John, are you more devoted to me than these others are?"

Peter said to me,

"Yes, Master, you know that I love you."

I said to him,

"Then feed my lambs!"

Again I said to him a second time,

"Simon, son of John, are you devoted to me?"

He said to me,

"Yes, Master, you know that I love you."

I said to him,

"Then be a shepherd to my sheep!"

I said to him a third time,

"Simon, son of John, do you love me?"

Peter was hurt because the third time I asked him if he loved me, and he answered,

"Master, you know everything, you can see that I love you."

I said to him,

"Then feed my sheep! I tell you, when you were young, you used to put on your own girdle and go where you pleased, but when you grow old, you will stretch out your hands and some-

one else will put a girdle on you and take you where you have
no wish to go."

I said this to show the kind of death by which Peter was to
honor God; and after I had said it I said to Peter,

"Follow me!"

Peter turned and saw following us the disciple who was very
dear to me, who at the supper leaned back on my breast and
said, "Master, who is it that is going to betray you?" When
Peter saw him, he said to me,

"But, Master, what about him?"

I said to him,

"If I wish him to wait till I come, what does it matter to
you? You must follow me."

So the story spread among the brothers that this disciple
was not going to die. But I did not tell him that he was not
going to die; I said, "If I wish him to wait till I come, what
does it matter to you?"

The Appearance to the Eleven on the Mountain

And the eleven disciples went to Galilee to the mountain
to which I had directed them. There they saw me and bowed
down before me, though some were in doubt about it.

And I came up to them and said,

"Full authority in heaven and on the earth has been given
to me. Therefore go and make disciples of all the heathen,
baptize them in the name of the Father, the Son, and the holy
Spirit, and teach them to observe all the commands that I
have given you. I will always be with you, to the very close of
the age."

I showed myself alive to them after I had suffered, in many
convincing ways, appearing to them through forty days and
telling them about the kingdom of God. And once when I ate
with my disciples I said: "This is what I told you when I was
still with you—that everything that is written about me in the

Law of Moses and the Prophets and the Psalms must come true."

Then I opened their minds to the understanding of the Scriptures, and said to them,

"The Scriptures said that the Christ should suffer as I have done, and rise the third day from the dead, and that repentance leading to the forgiveness of sins should be preached to all the heathen in my name. You are to be witnesses to all this, beginning at Jerusalem. And I will send down upon you what my Father has promised. Wait here in the city until you are clothed with power from on high."

When we were together on the Mount of Olives I told them: "John baptized people in water, but in a few days you will be baptized in the Holy Spirit." So those who were present asked me:

"Master, is this the time you are going to re-establish the kingdom for Israel?"

I said to them:

"It is not for you to know times and dates which the Father has fixed by his own authority, but you will be given power when the holy Spirit comes upon you, and you will be witnesses for me in Jerusalem and all over Judea and Samaria and to the very ends of the earth."

As I said this I was caught up before their eyes and a cloud took me out of their sight. While they were gazing after me into the sky, two men dressed in white suddenly stood before them, and said to them:

"Men of Galilee, why do you stand looking up into the sky? This very Jesus who has been caught up from you into heaven will come in just the way that you have seen him go up to heaven."

They went back to Jerusalem from the Mount of Olives to the upstairs room where they were staying. There were Peter, John, James and Andrew, Philip and Thomas, Bartholomew and Matthew, James the son of Alpheus, Simon the Zealot, and Judas the son of James. They were all devoting themselves with one mind to prayer, with the women and Mary, Jesus' mother, and his brothers.

On the day of the Harvest Festival, they were all meeting

together, when suddenly there came from the sky a sound like a violent blast of wind, and it filled the whole house where they were sitting. And they saw tongues like flames separating and settling on the head of each of them, and they were filled with the Holy Spirit and began to say in foreign languages whatever the spirit prompted them to utter.

There were devout Jews from every part of the world living in Jerusalem. When this sound was heard the crowd gathered in great excitement, because each one heard them speaking in his own language. They were perfectly amazed and said in their astonishment:

"Are not all these who are speaking Galileans? How then is it that each of us hears in his own tongue? Parthians, Medes, Elamites, residents of Mesopotamia, of Judea and Cappadocia, of Pontus and Asia, of Phrygia and Pamphylia, of Egypt and the district of Africa about Cyrene, visitors from Rome, Jews and proselytes, Cretans and Arabs—we all hear them tell in our own tongues the mighty deeds of God."

They were all amazed and bewildered and said to one another,

"What can this mean?" But others said derisively,

"They have had too much new wine."

Peter stood up with the eleven around him, and raising his voice addressed them,

"Men of Judea and all you residents of Jerusalem, let me explain this to you, and pay attention to what I say. These men are not drunk as you suppose, for it is only nine in the morning. But this is what was predicted by the prophet Joel:

It will come about in the last days, God says,
That I will pour out my spirit upon all mankind;
Your young men will have visions,
And your old men will have dreams. . . .
Then every one who calls upon the name of the Lord will be saved.

"Men of Israel, listen to what I say. Jesus of Nazareth, as you know, was a man whom God commended to you by the wonders, portents, and signs that God did right among you through him. But you, by the fixed purpose and intention of God, handed him over to wicked men, and had him crucified. But God raised him up from the dead, and to his resurrection we are all witnesses. God has declared this Jesus whom you crucified both Lord and Christ. You must repent, every one of you, and be baptized in the name of Jesus Christ in order to have your sins forgiven."

They welcomed his message and were baptized, and about three thousand people joined them that day.

There are many other things which I did, so many in fact that if they were all written out, I do not suppose that the world itself would hold the books that would have to be written. But these have been recorded so that you may believe that I am the Christ, the son of God, and through believing you may have life.